# In the Days of Jesus

Anthony J. Tambasco

# *In the Days of Jesus*

The Jewish Background
and
Unique Teaching of Jesus

*Paulist Press*  *New York/Ramsey*

Acknowledgement
*The Publisher gratefully acknowledges the use of the following material:*
Scripture texts used in this work are taken from the *New American Bible,* copyright © 1970, by the Confraternity of Christian Doctrine, Washington, D.C., and are used by permission of the copyright owner. All rights reserved.


*Maps by Frank Sabatté, C.S.P.*

Library of Congress
Catalog Card Number: 82-62919

ISBN: 0-8091-2536-6

Published by Paulist Press
545 Island Road, Ramsey, N.J. 07446

Printed and bound in the
United States of America

# *Contents*

Dedicated to _____

my Mother
and to the memory of my Dad

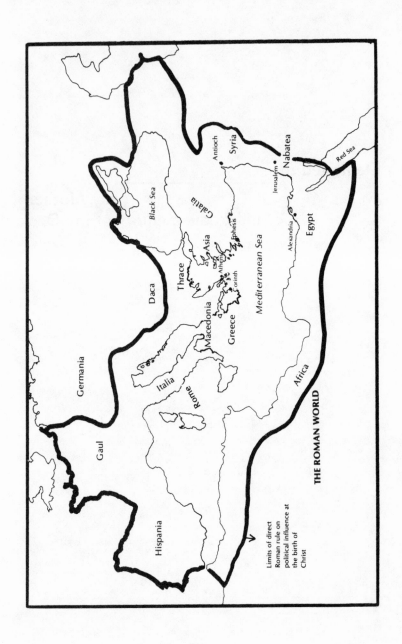

THE ROMAN WORLD

Limits of direct
Roman rule on
political influence at
the birth of
Christ

Hispania

Gaul

Germania

Italia

Rome

Daca

Thrace

Macedonia

Greece

Corinth

Athens

Asia

Ephesis

Black Sea

Galatia

Mediterranean Sea

Africa

Antioch

Syria

Jerusalem

Nabatea

Alexandria

Egypt

Red Sea

# *Preface*

I have always had a fascination for the Jesus of history. It seems to be a fascination shared by many, even if only out of our modern curiosity to get the facts on things. What was it like in the time of Jesus? What was Jesus really like? Did he really perform those miracles? Who actually put Jesus to death and on what charges? These points of curiosity are even more tantalizing for those who know that the Gospels cannot be read fundamentalistically as simple and factual biographies of Jesus. They are much more faith documents about who the risen Lord is, with a great deal of symbol, as we shall see.

Our concern in this book is to get behind the Gospel theology and symbols to the history of Jesus himself before his resurrection. This concern is not simply a matter of curiosity. The historical Jesus had his own particular message which forms the foundation for all that follows afterward. Study of the historical Jesus also gives us a sense of how much God entered into our human history and how he revealed himself in a gradual way through a genu-

1

ine human being. Without taking anything away from the divinity of Jesus it helps us to appreciate how he is like us in all things except sin.

My own fascination with the Jesus of history centers on two points which are the main concerns of this book: what is necessary from Jewish culture to understand Jesus, i.e., how much of a Jew was Jesus, and, secondly, what is unique about the teaching of Jesus, what makes him special. Both of these concerns put Jesus in the cultural milieu of his time and show how revelation builds into a gradual tradition. Jesus shows a great deal of continuity with his past Jewish traditions, even while he makes unique contributions that move him beyond them.

The method of study in this book is basically a documentary one. It tries simply to look at the first facts of Jesus, to show the cultural influences on the emerging Christian faith in its foundations, and to contrast cultural influences with those elements different and unique. Obviously, since Jesus made theological claims, even a study of the historical Jesus is not devoid of theological considerations. Nevertheless, these are presented simply as the claims of history without passing judgment. We are not doing a faith-reflection on religious history as such, nor is our concern to be evangelistic or apologetic.

Ultimately, of course, for one with faith this study can serve as encouragement. For one who believes in revelation it brings insight into the nature of that revelation. Still, this book is not directly a faith reflection. It tries to see what underlies any faith claim. It is simply a reflection on the foundational Christian story: Who was Jesus of Nazareth? What makes him so special? What would have been the historical experience of meeting Jesus in first century Palestine?

Since the method is documentary perhaps this book

will also serve as a first approach to Jesus for the outsider to Christianity or for the non-committed Christian. It may satisfy the curiosity over why so many make so much of Jesus and his message.

For whoever reads this book it is designed to be a crisp synopsis of the material. It is obviously not written for the scholar, but rather for the persons interested in knowing the conclusions of recent scholarship. The study stays in touch with that scholarship while not making the book heavy with footnotes and the details of research. The final product has been deliberately kept concise for those who wish a compact summary of this topic. I hope it will be of service to many who find this material of interest: the people involved with adult education, the pastoral ministers, the college undergraduates, the Christians seeking to learn more of their faith, the simply curious.

I would like to express thanks to my wife Joan for her encouragement and patience. I would also like to thank my colleagues at Georgetown University, Professors John Haught and Monika Hellwig, for their reading of the manuscript and for their helpful suggestions.

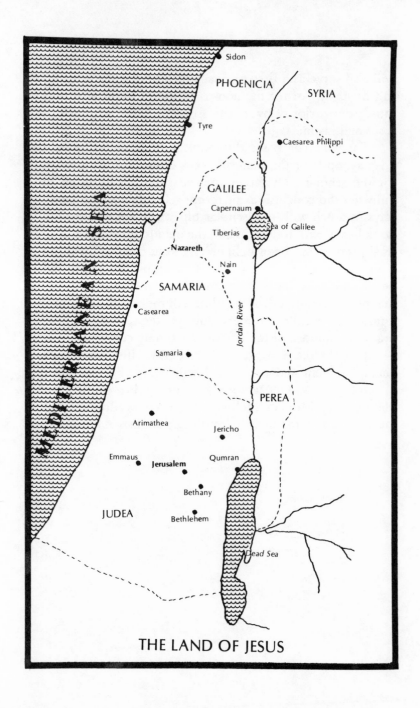

THE LAND OF JESUS

# Introduction

Because of the nature of Gospel literature, the search for the Jesus of history is not a simple matter of just reading the Gospels. Modern research has shown that while the Gospels may contain historical and biographical information they cannot be described as history books or biographies. The easiest way of determining this fact is to read particular Gospel texts carefully and to notice the discrepancies and even outright contradictions that exist if one were to take all the statements as historical fact.

For example, the infancy narratives appear only in Matthew and Luke and they are two entirely different stories. Moreover, the chronology of the accounts makes it impossible to harmonize the stories into one sequence of events. Likewise, if one compares John to any of the other three Synoptic Gospels, one finds almost an entirely different story of the life of Jesus. We try again to harmonize the two presentations, but that imposes an intention that the authors do not indicate as having, and it also glosses over some stories hard to reconcile.

In John, for instance, the cleansing of the temple takes place at the beginning of Jesus' career, in Chapter 2, whereas in the Synoptic Gospels the episode is toward the climax of Jesus' life near the end of the story. Only John gives the impression of three Passovers, indicating near to three years for Jesus' public life, while a Gospel like Luke's tries to make it a point that Jesus went to Jerusalem for one Passover only in his public life, so that his career seems closer to just one and a half years.

Individual stories are told differently in different Gospels. There are two different versions of the Lord's Prayer in Matthew 6 and Luke 11. The Beatitudes are different in Matthew 5 and Luke 6. Moreover, in Matthew Jesus goes *up* the mount to give his sermon, and the sermon is recorded as quite lengthy, embracing three whole chapters of the Gospel. In Luke Jesus comes *down* the mountain to a level plain and gives a considerably shorter discourse covering only part of one chapter. The sayings that are gathered in Matthew for the bulk of the Sermon on the Mount are either not found in Luke or are scattered throughout Luke's Gospel in varied historical contexts different from Matthew's.

The discrepancies can be multiplied enormously if one reads the Gospels carefully. One is left then with the option of saying that Jesus did things two or three times over with slight variations, or that the Gospel writers forgot the details. In the face of more and more discrepancies another option seems much more viable: none of the Gospel writers was interested in recording the straight historical facts, but had a different purpose in mind even if he was using the historical event in some way as a basis for the story.

The general intentions of the evangelists and the nature of Gospel literature can be better understood if we trace briefly the origins of the Gospels. These writings are the culmination of a substantial period of time in the early Church that was a period of intensive preaching and teaching. Jesus himself left no writings, and even the first apostles after the resurrection were not interested in writing. They were concerned rather with proclaiming good news. The word Gospel, which means good news, is better applied to this preaching by the first apostles before it can be applied to the written works. The written Gospels are chiefly the record of the oral tradition or preaching that preceded them.

When we inquire into the nature of the good news first preached by the apostles, we find it a simple statement, much the same as that expressed by Paul in 1 Corinthians 15:3-4, or in the speeches found interspersed throughout the Acts of the Apostles. Jesus died, but he is now risen. The good news is that Jesus is alive and present to us. When the first apostles went out to preach, they were concerned with telling people only that one important truth—that the resurrection had taken place.

The Jesus they were preaching was not the Jesus of the past, or simply the Jesus who left a wonderful message. The Jesus they were preaching was the Jesus who could truly be called the Christ, because he was alive and active and present with new power for the audience who were listening to the preaching. The distinction is worth repeating: the apostles were interested in answering the question, "Who *is* Jesus, alive and present to us?" and not the question which for them was secondary and unimportant, "Who *was* Jesus?"

Very quickly, however, the early preachers needed to fill in their picture more elaborately. It was fine to tell people the simple fact that Jesus was alive and risen. Yet the congregations wanted to know more about this risen

Lord and what he meant. Gradually the preachers devised a method of filling in the picture. They went back to the public life of Jesus, to what he said and did, in order to give a fuller idea of who the risen Jesus might be. Little by little stories of Jesus became part of the good news or the oral Gospel.

Notice, however, the use of the stories taken from the public life of Jesus. When the preachers went back to these historical events, they used them not in order to say what went on "back then," but to shed light on what was going on right in the present with the experience of the risen Lord. They took sayings and actions of Jesus to show what he was still saying and doing in the present. Even when the first apostles went back to the Jesus of history it was not to answer the questions, "Who *was* Jesus? What *did* he say and do then?" but rather to answer yet the question, "Who *is* Jesus, still saying and doing what he said and did in the past?"   ·

Because the early apostles had selective purpose in going back to the stories of the historical Jesus, several things happened to these stories. First of all, the preachers were selective in the stories they used. They did not go back to all the events of the historical Jesus. They used only those sayings and events that shed light on who the risen Jesus was for their own audiences. Thus, we no longer have a full biography of Jesus, since no one was interested or found it useful to preserve one for us. We have only that assortment of episodes that shed light on the first proclamation of the good news of the resurrection.

As time went on in the oral tradition, moreover, these episodes tended to be isolated from each other and from their historical context. A saying of Jesus, for example, or a parable would be used to make a point. As it proved useful it would be used over and over until eventually no one remembered quite exactly when Jesus originally uttered the saying. Sometimes the same saying would serve different messages and would be used differently. (Look, for example, at the use of the saying in Matthew 19:30, and then in Matthew 20:16, and then the same saying in Luke 13:30.)

By the time we get to the written Gospel we have hardly any chronological biography of Jesus, but rather a string of stories which have the important theological purpose of reclaiming the meaning of the risen Lord. Of course, the general chronology of the life of Jesus is retained, but the particular details and the juxtaposition of events are much more the work of oral tradition and the Gospel writers than of the actual historical Jesus. Once again, it makes it difficult to reconstruct a simple, factual biography of Jesus.

Another decisive step was taken with the stories of the public life of Christ that also removed them from simple biography. The early preachers found that the sayings and the events from the public life of Jesus were actually inadequate to convey the fuller theology of the risen Lord. The resurrection of Christ not only confirmed the previous teaching of Jesus. It advanced that teaching and gave new revelation. For all of its depth the preaching of the Jesus of history had to be incomplete, simply because some things could not be said until Jesus rose from the dead. How, for instance, could Jesus even talk about his second coming until it was clear to people what his first coming would achieve? How, for instance, could Jesus say anything about the nature of the Church as his presence in the world until he rose and showed people how he could be present in the world today?

Since the early apostles found that there was not enough material from the public life of Jesus to get across their message, but since they were using the format of stories from the life of Jesus, they determined to continue that format, but to modify it. They continued to tell sayings and events from the life of Jesus. However, when need arose to give a deeper teaching, they added a saying or an event, or they changed around or reinterpreted a saying or event in order to shed full light on the risen Jesus.

The semblance of a biography of Jesus was simply the format or vehicle for their conveying truth. They felt free to claim that Jesus said or did something, not because that actually happened historically, but because they knew it to be the truth that the risen Lord was saying or doing in the present. What they were presenting was truly from Jesus Christ, even if not necessarily from the Jesus of past history.

Such use of the stories of Jesus for preaching in the oral tradition shows how problematic it is to get to the simple biography of the historical Jesus. One must abstract it from what has been added, changed, reinterpreted or removed from its historical context. That was the case already in the very first preaching and in the oral tradition of the first Christians. The written Gospel is the record of that preaching, and so the problem has simply been transferred to the Gospels as we have them. That accounts for the discrepancies and the contradictions that we have mentioned above, and that accounts for why we said there was a problem in searching for the Jesus of history.

Of course, reading the Gospels is no problem at all if one is simply in tune with the major purpose of each writer and if one approaches the text as a faith proclamation of the risen Lord. The problem arises for us in this particular study because we are concerned with a secondary issue that can come only indirectly from the Gospels and that it was not their main purpose to give. Nevertheless, it is worth tackling the problem because it helps us see the foundational theology and the starting point for all that the Gospels eventually become. It also gives insight into the person of Jesus himself.

Biblical scholars have offered a number of criteria to help discern the historical material of the Gospels, and we will look at them briefly in order to know what principles are operating behind the portrait that we will draw of the Jesus of history. First of all, there is the criterion of dissimilarity. This tool helps us to isolate at least what is unique to the historical Jesus. It operates on the assumption that if a saying or event has no meaning or direct theological relevance for the early Christian Church, then it probably originates out of the time of Jesus himself. On the other hand, if a saying or event makes more sense as explaining a theological point for the early Church, and makes less sense as coming out of Jesus' time and culture, then that saying or event probably originates in the oral tradition and does not belong to the historical Jesus.

This principle helps us recognize that many texts make more sense in the hindsight of the resurrection than they do for the historical Jesus, and helps us eliminate a number of passages as not historical. Among other things, this criterion suggests that we eliminate any teaching on the divinity of Jesus, anything that would look like theology later developed by a Church expanding to the Gentiles, and anything that would presuppose a fully formed community of Christian believers. All these concerns would make more sense as later insights as a result of the resurrection of Jesus. They would be premature as teaching of the historical Jesus.

The criterion of dissimilarity would encourage us to recognize and to take seriously the humanity of Jesus.

However, it would only lead us to detect those elements in the human life of Jesus where he moved beyond his traditions and offered new insights to humanity. We will use the results of this criterion to outline what is unique about the historical Jesus and what serves as the foundational theology for all that follows. The principle, by its very nature, will not be helpful in deciphering what Jesus has in common with the Jewish culture around him and what he has in common with the early Church after his resurrection.

To uncover the cultural background of Jesus and his Jewish roots, we will use the criterion of multiple attestation. This principle presumes that if a particular theme or concern arises in a number of different Gospel traditions or elsewhere in the New Testament or if a particular theme occurs within varied literary forms in one Gospel (e.g., a parable, a saying and an event), then it has high probability of being historical in the public life of Jesus. Because of the multiple attestation we can include a number of things that we might otherwise eliminate because they could have come from the Jewish culture around the first converts after the resurrection in Palestine. Rather than excluding these themes we can conclude that Jesus built on the Jewish culture around him and that this culture continued right into the early Church.

Another criterion that can be of secondary help to the others is the criterion of linguistic and environmental tests. This principle helps us to link Jesus to his Jewish culture by eliminating anything that seems incompatible with the language or the environment of his own ministry. A final secondary criterion is that of consistency. This presumes that any saying or event in the Gospel can be accepted as from the historical Jesus if it is consistent with the total outlook of the historical Jesus as determined from the other criteria.

As one can see, we must proceed cautiously and with conclusions that remain more or less tentative. There is endless debate among scholars over particular passages of the Gospels. We certainly will not be able to put together a detailed biography of Jesus. We can have, however, a general portrait. There is surprising agreement over the main thrust of the life of the historical Jesus. We can construct an exciting picture of his Jewish background, of the unique features of this man Jesus, and of the theology of his public life that provided the foundation for all later theology.

## *Suggestions for Additional Reading:*

McEleney, Neil J. *Growth of the Gospels.* Paulist Press, 1979.

Marrow, Stanley B. *Words of Jesus in Our Gospels.* Paulist Press, 1979.

Jeremias, Joachim. *The Problem of the Historical Jesus.* Fortress/ Facet Books, 1964.

# Coming of Age in Galilee

## Suggested Scripture Readings:

| Matthew | Luke |
|---------|------|
| 4:12–25 | 2:1–52 |
| 9:9 | 12:13–21 |
| 13:1–9; 53–58 | 13:1–5 |
| 20:1–16 | |

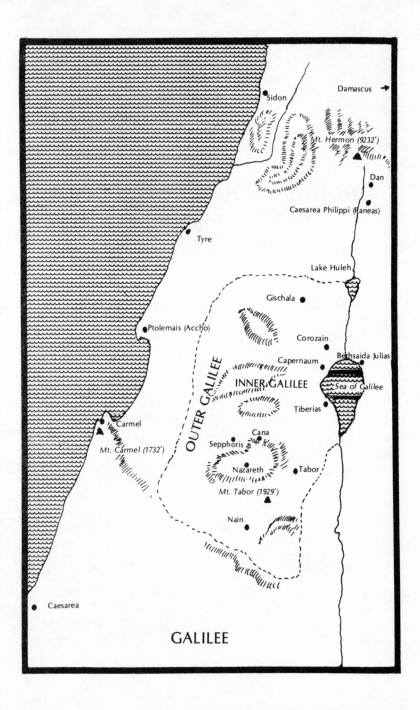

Sidon

Damascus →

Mt. Hermon (9232')

Dan

Caesarea Philippi (Paneas)

Tyre

Lake Huleh

Gischala

Corozain

Capernaum

Bethsaida Julias

Ptolemais (Accho)

INNER GALILEE

Sea of Galilee

OUTER GALILEE

Tiberias

Cana

Carmel

Sepphoris

Nazareth

Tabor

Mt. Carmel (1732')

Mt. Tabor (1929')

Nain

Caesarea

GALILEE

The center stage for the beginning of the life of Jesus is Galilee and its towns with names over-familiar to Christians: Nazareth, Naim, Cana, Capernaum. Here we find the Jewish roots of Jesus and the foundations of his career. He would continue Jewish tradition even while he made unique contributions to it. As far as concerns the birth and the early years of Jesus prior to his public life, we have unfortunately no substantial direct information.

The infancy narratives appear only in the Gospels of Matthew and Luke, and even these seem for the most part to be quite elaborate theological reinterpretations of Jesus in the hindsight of his resurrection. The two infancy stories are almost entirely different from each other and point to their symbolic meaning rather than historical accuracy. At best we can probably conclude from these stories that Jesus was born in Bethlehem but spent his life in Nazareth. He was born of Mary, espoused to a man named Joseph. The historicity of the rest of the narratives remains problematic, though one or another of the points may still be debated.

From texts found later in the Gospels we also can assume as historical the occupation of Jesus as the carpenter's son and the listing of James, Joses, Judas and Simon as his close relatives along with some women. Whether they are literally brothers and sisters, or actually cousins, is left open to debate as far as the biblical text is concerned, since both meanings are possible from the word to describe them. For our information on the cultural background of Jesus beyond these meager facts, we will have to rely on the non-biblical literature of the time and on archeological discoveries of our own day. Fortunately these are not wanting, and we can draw a good general portrait of the Jewish background from which Jesus begins his career.

The story of the historical Jesus unfolds in the territory of Galilee, a name which means "circle" and aptly describes the region forming a circle around the land somewhat north, west and south of the Sea of Galilee on its eastern frontier. It is a land of hill country, consisting mostly of villages and hamlets, largely of a rural quality. The entire territory forms the northern part of the land of Palestine. A faint shadow of the glory of the Old Testament, this northern portion was now separated from Judea with its city Jerusalem in the south. Between them lay the territory of Samaria, whose inhabitants were no longer considered by Galileans and Judeans as rightful descendants of the Jewish heritage. The Samaritans had diluted Judaism through intermarriage with pagans and were now the object of scorn of Galilee and Judea.

In many ways Galilee was different from Jerusalem and Judea, and the geographic situation of the territory was a major factor in that difference. Actually, even Galilee itself was of two kinds of geography. The entire area was fertile and given to farming. However, the inner regions of the circle were isolated by hills and ravines, much less accessible to outside influence than the level coastal areas and plains on the western, southern and eastern parts of the outer circle. The rich farming made Galilee different from cosmopolitan but barren Jerusalem. The difference in Galilee itself between hills and plains made it possible to speak of an inner Galilee and an outer Galilee.

The entire territory of the north had known foreign oppression for a long time in its history. During the time of Jesus the tyrant was Rome, but more directly the Herodian kings who ruled by favor of Rome. Herod the Great was granted the monarchy about forty years before the time of Jesus and ruled over both Galilee and Judea until he died shortly after the birth of Jesus. When he died the territories over which he ruled were divided among his sons, and Herod Antipas succeeded to the throne in Galilee. Since he, like his father, was only partly Jewish, he was considered foreign by the Jews. He brought some stability and external peace to the area, but at the price of heavy taxation which classified him easily as an oppressor.

The rule of the Herods brought as the greatest danger the Hellenistic culture of the Roman empire which posed the threat of pagan influence upon the Jewish religion. Galilee did not generally succumb to this new culture as did Samaria, but the responses of the Jews varied, especially from outer to inner Galilee. In the outlying, more accessible areas the Gentile influence was felt more keenly. Urban life developed more rapidly. There was either more pointed acceptance or rejection of the new cultural influences. Some Jews compromised their religion as much as they considered possible and joined the Gentiles in their Hellenistic way of life. They earned the nickname for the territory, "Galilee of the Gentiles."

Others saw more clearly the threat of Herod's lifestyle and spoke of revolution and radical overthrow of the Roman taskmasters. Galilee developed the reputation of housing bandits and revolutionaries, a reputation partially true and an eventuality that did ultimately lead to the destruction of the Jewish nation altogether after the time of Jesus. The strong sentiments for or against Herod gave rise to the Herodians and the Zealots respectively. These groups were known by Jesus in his lifetime and are mentioned in the Gospels (cf. Mk 3:6 and Lk 13:1).

The Jews of inner Galilee, on the other hand, had much milder reactions to Herod and were more conservative and traditional in their political viewpoints. In this rugged area, isolated from the urban centers, people were generally unaware of the great cultural changes taking place in the surrounding territory. They were more concerned with their day to day tasks of agriculture and were not caught up in other issues. They knew that being under foreign powers was a fact of life, but were indifferent to who that might be as long as they were left with their agriculture and ties to the land. They were committed to their religion as a firm tradition, but in resignation they saw no need to be revolutionary to keep the tradition. They did, of course, have as much oppression as the rest of Galilee, but the idea of revolution would have to be carried to these reactionary hamlets from the outside before they joined in the sentiments of the rest of Jewish Galilee.

The conservatism and slow rate of change in the inner territory also accounted for primitive agriculture itself and the poverty of the townsfolk. At the same time the oppression of Herod and the Herodians showed in farming itself and accounted for the poor quality of life in both the inner and the outer regions of Galilee. In the little villages and hamlets there was farming more by way of family loyalty and fidelity to ancestral ways than by concern for more wealth or a better standard of living. These townsfolk were not aware of new methods of irrigation and new methods of farming that were being imported by Hellenistic culture. Jesus himself makes us aware of the simpler farming methods when he tells the story of the sower who went out and planted his crop by the somewhat primitive method still of scattering the seed at random about the field. Nor was there much advance planning. Farming depended on the vagaries of the weather and on an uncertain market. If crops failed, there was famine. If there was an overabundance, the market value dropped to the advantage of large farm aristocrats who could handle a smaller profit margin.

The creation of large farms was the way in which the ruling class reinforced the poverty in the hamlets and even in the outer, more developed areas. In the most fertile and readily accessible plains and valleys, especially in the Plain of Esdraelon between Galilee and Samaria, Herod confiscated the land and gave it to his supporters. The aristocracy then hired out the land to tenant farmers and day laborers who grew produce which they could scarcely keep for themselves.

In the interior regions of Galilee Herod allowed the small, individually owned farms to exist independently, but he appropriated them if the owners defaulted on debts or taxes. At the first crisis the poor farmer had to borrow and most often went deeper and deeper into debt. The eventual result was the creation of many absentee landlords among the Herodians who controlled more and more tenant farmers. In any case the farmer who owned his land was not really much different in his poor standard of living from the tenant farmer. Jesus makes reference in his parables to the stewards who administered the lands, often unjustly, for their absentee masters (Lk 16:1–6; Mt 24:45–57).

Besides farming as the major occupation, fishing served as a major industry because of the availability of the Sea of Galilee, the only fresh water lake in Palestine. Unfortunately, even the fishermen and the associated tradesmen were kept in poverty. The fee for fishing rights was quite high. Moreover, the sale of fish and fish products was farmed out by Herod to middlemen who marketed to their own advantage, with little left for the fishermen themselves.

When we consider the specific occupation of Jesus in his younger life, we find that carpentry belonged to the category of all the other trades established in a village according to need. These trades were not major industries, nor could they even be considered skills of a middle class, such as the craftsmen who are considered artisans in the Acts of the Apostles. The craftsmen of Galilee were there to meet local need. They kept their roots with the peasant culture and played minor roles to the major activity of fishing and farming. For the most part they were as poor as the rest. There simply was no middle class in Galilee. Along with carpentry we can imagine other necessary trades such as shepherding, sandal-making, shopkeeping, shearing and tanning. The women, of course, were given to cooking and baking, spinning and weaving.

All in all, then, there were two classes of society where Jesus lived and grew up. There were the Herodians and the landed aristocracy, and then there were the poor tied to the land, whether as small landowners just out of debt or as hired help or as craftsmen in service of these peasant farmers. So much was this experience a part of the life of Jesus that it came forth spontaneously to illustrate his later preaching. He spoke of rich men who had stewards and poor men who owed them much (Lk 16:1–6; Mt 18:23–34; Lk 7:41). He talked of vineyard owners who hired day laborers or who leased the land to tenant farmers (Mt 20:1–16; 21:33–41). He talked of rich fools who wanted to hoard their wealth by building larger granaries (Lk 12:13–21). He knew of family farms where sons had to share the inheritance (Lk 15:11–31) or where the father needed the help of his sons in the vineyards (Mt 21:28–32). Jesus not only knew of these people. He identified with the poor class and would later have things to say about the poor and about the ruling authorities.

There was one other group of people whom Jesus knew from his earliest years and who would be the object of his concern later on. These were the tax collectors. Obviously, taxes were a heavy burden throughout Galilee. There were religious taxes for the priests and the temple in Jerusalem. What was far worse, however, was the system of secular taxes. Herod imposed not only a land tax, but also a toll tax, i.e., a fee that had to be paid whenever one moved merchandise from one district to another. The tolls helped insure poverty, for they discouraged people from moving to better places for market or for resources.

These taxes also led to a group of people who knew the hostility of the Jews. Herod farmed out his collection of taxes. Social climbers welcomed the opportunity to collect the taxes, since it helped to bring them into the rich class. Some of these social climbers were Jews who became collaborators. To make matters worse, the tax collecting became itself a further oppression. Herod arranged that the collectors were responsible for deficits, but could keep the extra that they collected. It was an incentive for some to collect unjust taxes for further profit. It was a brave Jesus who would overcome this hostility later on, welcoming tax collectors and even making Matthew one of his twelve intimate disciples.

Closely connected with the political and cultural ethos of Galilee was its religious climate. Politics and culture affected the way Galileans looked at their religion, and religion helped them to deal with politics and culture. The greatest influence, undoubtedly, on Jesus was a firm Judaism, intact perhaps because Galilee felt threatened by Samaria. Samaritans had long ago diluted their Judaism with pagan practices. Galilee felt a threat to do the same. Yet this undiluted Judaism knew different tendencies which Jesus would wrestle with and which would take on clearer delineation as he moved toward Jerusalem in his public life.

Galilee was famous for its apocalyptic expectations, that is, its looking forward to the culmination of history and the final arrival of God's triumph over evil and the full redemption of Israel. Still, this apocalyptic mood was prevalent among only some of the Galileans, especially those in the urban and more accessible areas. It accompanied the Zealot movements which looked forward to the final overthrow of Herod's evil reign and the liberation of the land.

Among the more traditional inner regions of Galilee the faith was more simply tied to the land. The peasants thanked God for the blessings of the land and were content enough with the status quo, since they felt that things could be worse. Their thanks for the land was linked to the temple theology of Jerusalem, since the God of the temple was seen as the God who gave the land. They accepted the tithe for the temple as a tax, even if poverty prevented their paying it all the time.

Devotion to the temple lay behind the fidelity of the Galileans to the yearly pilgrimages to Jerusalem. They were asked to go for the feasts of Passover, Pentecost and Tabernacles, though their finances usually allowed just the pilgrimage for Passover. They celebrated the festivals nonetheless. Passover commemorated the exodus from Egypt; Pentecost, at wheat harvest, recalled the giving of the law on Sinai; Tabernacles celebrated the fruit harvest and included the Day of Atonement and festivals of joy and light.

Luke recalls in his infancy text that Mary and Joseph joined the caravans making the three day journey to Jerusalem for Passover, and says that Jesus went with them because he was at the transitional age of twelve. The details of the story are probably reflection of later theology but the fact of the journey is probable, based on the way of life that would have been customary in Galilee. Later in his public life Jesus will again go to Jerusalem for the feasts, as his religious upbringing taught him.

The mainstay and the center of religious life in Galilee was the synagogue. There was only one temple and that was in Jerusalem. The regular religious nourishment had to come locally from the synagogue or meeting place where the Scriptures could be read and preached and prayers could be offered. This institution grew out of Israel's time in the Babylonian exile, when she needed a substitute for the temple which lay in ruins in Jerusalem. The synagogue became a regular institution from that time onward, even after the temple was rebuilt.

The non-sacrificial ritual of the synagogue (sacrifices were offered only in the temple) began with the call to worship and the reading of the *Shema,* the text from Deuteronomy 6:4, "Hear, O Israel: The Lord our God is one Lord; and you shall love the Lord your God with all your

heart, and with all your soul, and with all your might."
Then after blessings and prayers, there was a reading from
the Torah or law, i.e., a text from one of the first five
books of the Old Testament which are considered the
most sacred to Israel's Bible. A second reading would
come from the prophets, followed by a sermon or exhortation and then concluding with a blessing.

During the service the men would sit in the center of
the room faced by the rabbi, cantors, and other leaders
who were sitting up front. The women and children
would be around the sides and in the rear. Occasionally a
guest rabbi or even a layman from the congregation
would give the exhortation. In just such a setting, Jesus
undoubtedly heard much of his Scripture, and when he
began his public life he would himself do the speaking in
such synagogue services (cf. Lk 4:16–30).

So we have the quality of life and the setting of first
century Palestine out of which the historical Jesus
emerged. Jesus' life in Galilee would be experienced first
in the context of his own family and then in his movement
into his own life in young adulthood; finally it would be
the starting point for his public life. Jesus would have
been born into a family which had strong Jewish convictions. Joseph would have been serious about his obligations to support the family and to teach Torah and a trade
to Jesus. When Jesus was eight days old he would have
been circumcised as a sign of his being part of the people
of God. Mary would have been entrusted with the early
years and training of her son, but as he grew to manhood
Joseph would have taken over. When Jesus was about thir-
teen he would have been considered as moving into manhood and would then gradually assume responsibilities of
an adult in the Jewish faith.

Besides the training that he received at home, Jesus

would have learned from the setting around him. He would hear the elders discussing at the gates of the village. He would hear the conversations at the well of the city and especially when caravans were forming. Eventually he would even be part of them. Most of all, Jesus would be formed by the liturgies in the synagogue and would hear the Word of God and the explanations from the preachers sabbath after sabbath.

In addition to his religious training, and while he was learning these things, Jesus would, as the first-born learn to read and most likely to write. The informal education of his society would be the heritage which he possessed as he left Nazareth to begin his public life. He used much of what he learned in his own message and remained, as we shall see, firmly rooted in his Jewish traditions. However, he also moved beyond these roots to establish his own unique teaching. We must now move to his public life and the gradual unfolding of the message of the historical Jesus.

## *Suggestions for Additional Reading:*

Bruce, Frederick F. *New Testament History.* Doubleday, 1969.

Brown, Raymond. *An Adult Christ at Christmas.* Liturgical Press, 1978.

———. *The Virginal Conception and Bodily Resurrection of Jesus.* Paulist Press, 1973.

Freyne, Seán. *Galilee, from Alexander the Great to Hadrian, 323 B.C.E. to 135 C.E.: A Study of Second Temple Judaism.* Michael Glazier and University of Notre Dame Press, 1980. (A more thorough, but more specialized work.)

McHugh, John. "The Brothers of Jesus," in *The Mother of Jesus in the New Testament.* Doubleday, 1975, Part II, Chapters 6–9.

# Up to Jerusalem

## Suggested Scripture Readings:

| Mark | Luke |
|------|------|
| 7:1–8 | 13:31–35 |
| 12:18–34 | 21:1–3 |
| 13:1–2 | |

### John

5:1–9
11:45–53

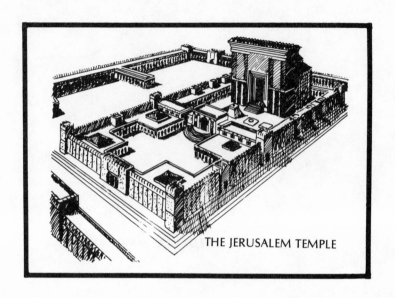

THE JERUSALEM TEMPLE

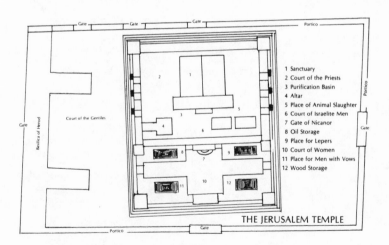

1 Sanctuary
2 Court of the Priests
3 Purification Basin
4 Altar
5 Place of Animal Slaughter
6 Court of Israelite Men
7 Gate of Nicanor
8 Oil Storage
9 Place for Lepers
10 Court of Women
11 Place for Men with Vows
12 Wood Storage

THE JERUSALEM TEMPLE

The Judaism from which Jesus emerged and to which he spoke was a Judaism that took its major characteristics from Jerusalem in Judea. The Judaism of Galilee had its mentor in Jerusalem. Jesus would have traveled there on pilgrimage. Here was the cultural and political capital of Jewish Palestine and the religious capital of all of Judaism. The social and cultural background of the city was again influenced in large part by its geographic location, but for Jerusalem the social and cultural background also influenced the geographical limitations.

Geographically Jerusalem was not well situated for the cosmopolitan character that it had and for its being the hub of Jewish Palestine. It was in the hill country somewhat similar to the inner core of Galilee, but Jerusalem was much more barren. There was some better land to the west along the coastal area of the Mediterranean, but it was separated from the city by ravines and rugged territory. There were no natural passes east-west through Jerusalem. To the east lay mostly desert area, with the Dead

Sea and its surrounding desert off to the southeast, and the same kind of terrain with only an occasional oasis like Jericho off to the northeast. Jerusalem was more adapted to be a fortress than a central capital city.

Nevertheless, a thriving cosmopolitan city is what it was from the time that David conquered the Jebusites and set it up as his religious and political capital. Access to the city was created artificially and was sustained by the respect which all of Judaism held for the city. Jerusalem thrived because of its social and cultural position as a religious capital and as a political center.

Economically the city was dependent on imports for all of its existence. There was perhaps a minimum of olive oil that could be produced from the groves in Gethsemane across the valley to the east of the city. Otherwise Jerusalem had to import just about everything. Of special importance, of course, were wheat and livestock, but many other raw materials and finished products were also brought in for the large population.

One of the factors that encouraged the trade and became responsible for much of the economic life of the city was the religious institution of the temple. Revenue came in because of the daily needs of the temple, because of the foreign traffic that arrived for the major annual feasts, because of temple taxes, and because of the wealthy who eventually settled in the city for religious purposes.

From the time of Herod the Great just prior to the birth of Jesus the temple was being reconstructed, enlarged and beautified. It was a long process of completing the temple that had been constructed after the return from the Babylonian exile. Its major task employed people for years, artisans that numbered in the tens of thousands. Trades flourished in architecture, masonry, stonecutting, carpentry, metalwork, goldsmithing, etc. Auxiliary trades grew up for the support of this massive community of temple builders.

In addition to these construction needs, the temple also had its daily requirements for normal function. There were the bakers of the loaves of proposition which were symbolic offerings put in the temple sanctuary. There were incense makers, weavers and knitters for huge temple curtains and the veil of the temple which separated the sanctuary from the Holy of Holies in the rear of the building. There were goldsmiths, moneychangers to give Jewish coins in exchange for pagan money for the temple taxes, merchants of sheep and doves for sacrifice. There was even a temple doctor and barbers for purification rites of lepers and for those taking special vows in the temple.

Jerusalem swelled in population for the festivals, especially for Passover, so that buying and selling reached enormous proportions. To help that along there were also some religious prescriptions. For Passover itself all the Jews were to be inside the city of Jerusalem. So crowded were conditions that it was necessary to consider the city as legally extending to outlying areas such as Bethany. Jesus himself is described as having spent the evenings of his last Passover in these outlying areas. Obviously merchants came along with the pilgrims and trade flourished. In addition the law required not only that pilgrims pay the tithe to the temple and priests, but that they spend a "second tithe" by purchases within the city of Jerusalem during the pilgrimage.

The cultural importance of the city was complemented by its political importance. From Jerusalem ruled the central council of the Jews which at least in theory was said to be the policy-maker of all of Judaism. Its political authority was considerably weak in Galilee and almost non-existent among Jews in the dispersion, but it was powerful in Judea. The council was called the Sanhedrin and consisted of seventy members. At the head was the high priest, chosen from among the priests for one year, but sometimes wielding authority even after his term expired. We know that Annas continued to have power during the last days of Jesus, while his son-in-law Caiaphas actually had the office. Along with the high priest ruled the priestly aristocracy and the elders, who were lay property owners in the city. Finally scribes were admitted also to the council. These were also laymen who were proficient in the Torah or scrolls of the law and taught it in the synagogues and temple area. The scribe was known as the rabbi, which simply means "master" or teacher.

The Sanhedrin was given much autonomy for the political jurisdiction of Jerusalem and for religious governance, but Roman authority also made its presence felt. Since Jerusalem was the center of Palestine for the Jews, the Romans kept watch there. Herod the Great was given jurisdiction and built a palace there even though he had also built an entire Hellenistic city in Caesarea on the Mediterranean coast. When Herod died, Judea was left to his son Archelaus. So badly did the latter rule that he was deposed while Jesus was still a small child, and the Romans ruled directly through a procurator who was subject in turn to Caesar's legate residing in Syria. Pontius Pilate held the post during Jesus' career. These rulers added an additional burden upon Jerusalem in the form of taxes as well as political domination.

The larger world into which Jesus eventually moved and which he must have experienced on pilgrimages was quite cosmopolitan, in some ways similar to his native Galilee and in some ways quite different. Similar to Galilee would be the existence of the rich and the poor, but in Jerusalem there was also the middle class. The aristocracy grew around the Herod family and the Herodians and showed wealth in homes, clothes and slaves and even sometimes in extravagant and insincere gifts to the temple. In Jerusalem, however, there was also an aristocracy among the priests of the temple. We notice at the trial of Jesus, for instance, that the high priestly residence contained a large courtyard with doorkeeper and servants, as well as the granaries for the wheat tithes.

The middle class came not from industry so much as from trade. There were no farmers or fishermen as in Galilee, but there were numerous merchants, and in Jerusalem they could acquire enough wealth to establish a middle class. They imported goods and traded them in the bazaars of the market, with different trades in different bazaars. We also find that some of the artisans and craftsmen could enter the middle class by owning their own premises and by not hiring themselves out. The middle class grew especially for the middlemen who negotiated the conveniences of pilgrims for the temple, e.g., bakers, tavern keepers, caterers, and clothiers.

The poor were a landless group in Jerusalem. They may have hired themselves out as laborers, but most of them were on relief. Curiously enough, the ordinary priests and the scribes were often in this class, when the tithes did not make it down to the lower echelons of the priestly caste and when the scribes did not have artisan skills to support their other work of teaching and interpreting Scripture. The blind, lame and similar unfortunates of the poor were found begging in great numbers at the city gates, the outer courts of the temple, and the great pools like that of Bethesda and the pool of Siloam. There was a great dole to feed paupers daily and there was a weekly dole for food and clothing. Charity was promoted as a meritorious work, but much of it was done either with a sense of self-righteousness or for external show. Jesus absorbed this experience and would include it when later he talked about the real meaning of justice and when he had to exhort the rich and the middle class to care for the poor. And in Jerusalem the aristocracy which he criticized would have to include religious authorities as well as Roman.

When one moves from the socio-economic and the political complexion of Jerusalem to its religious schools of thought one encounters a variety of viewpoints. Here we find the official centers of the varied opinions that were lived in an informal way in Galilee. Jesus would have had to grapple with this theology more and more intensely as he grew into greater awareness of all that came from Jerusalem. Most significant of all the thinkers were the two rival sects of the Sadducees and the Pharisees. It might be fairer to call them tendencies rather than sects, since they represented the two main tendencies of Judaism of the time.

The Sadducees were uncompromising literalists of the law. They held fast to Torah but only to what could be seen in the letter of the law. They had their own scribes to advocate their particular interpretations and rejected anything that was seen as developing doctrine in the traditions but was not located explicitly in the texts. Thus, they would not accept resurrection of the dead, personal immortality and retribution after death. They applied the lex talionis, i.e., "an eye for an eye," literally, whereas Pharisees saw mitigating circumstances.

Since most of the Sadducees were priests, their theology centered heavily on the importance of the temple and sacrifice in Jerusalem. They were also strongly interested in the tithing to support the temple and themselves. Logically enough, the Sadducees were the religious aristocracy, and so their political views tended to be favorable toward the status quo of their society. Since they had the most to lose they sought as much compromise as possible with the Roman authorities and with the extreme group of Herodians.

The Pharisees were at the other end of the controversies. They were mostly laymen and centered their attention on the law. However, their interpretation of the law allowed for updating and new developments in tradition beyond the literal text. Our Gospels put them in a more unfavorable light than was actually the case, probably because of later Jewish-Christian polemic. Most of the scribes were Pharisees, and Pharisaism was the predominant movement in Judaism, even if inner Galilee was more favorable to a Sadducean viewpoint than a Pharisaic one.

Concern with the law brought the Pharisees to emphasize ritual purity and holiness of life. They believed in an afterlife and personal retribution. On the positive side they promoted love for the Torah for holiness. On the negative side they became involved in much casuistry. Their interpretations of law allowed for new viewpoints and updating, but sometimes this led them to piling law upon law. Finally, unlike the Sadducees, the Pharisees had little to lose by more separatist views, and so they advocated opposition to Hellenism and foreign rule. Their position would find a hearing among those groups in Galilee who opposed oppression and carried opposition to even more radical theories of revolution.

Besides these two main tendencies in Jerusalem there were also other sects that advocated radical reform in Judaism. One large sect was that of the Essenes, not mentioned in the Bible but known through recent archeology. These sectarians broke off from Jerusalem, becoming more radical separatists than the Pharisees, but not violent like the Zealots. They considered the priesthood of Jerusalem so corrupt that it was beyond repair, so they moved to form their own communities that would try to live the law more purely and that would provide the context for God's final redemption of Israel.

One prominent Essene group lived in a monastery in the desert by the Dead Sea. This community at Qumran admitted members only after two years of probation. The members pooled their resources and lived by manual labor, by study of the scrolls of the Bible and their own writings, and by their own unique rituals. Included in the rituals were sacred common meals, sabbath observance, and purification rites. Sects like the Essenes fostered a climate of expectation of God's final work and contributed in their own way to the apocalyptic expectations of the time. Out of this climate stepped John the Baptist who would provide the final context for Jesus' own arrival.

## Suggestions for Additional Reading:

Tricot, Alphonse. "The Jewish World," in André Robert and André Feuillet, eds. *Introduction to the New Testament.* Desclee Co, 1965, Introduction, Section II, Chapters 1–2.

Bruce, Frederick F. *New Testament History.* Doubleday, 1969.

Mackowski, Richard M. (text) and Nalbandian, Garo (photos). *Jerusalem, City of Jesus.* Eerdmans, 1980.

Jeremias, Joachim. *Jerusalem in the Time of Jesus.* Fortress, 1969. (A scholarly work, but a major reference tool.)

Safrai, S. and Stern, M., eds. *The Jewish People in the First Century.* 2 vols. Fortress, 1974/76. (A scholarly compendium of all aspects of Jewish history and culture.)

# *The Baptist and His Message*

## *Suggested Scripture Readings:*

*Matthew*

3:1–17
11:1–19

*Mark*

2:18–22
6:14–29

*Luke*

1:1–80
7:18–35

*John*

1:6–8, 15, 19–42
3:22–30

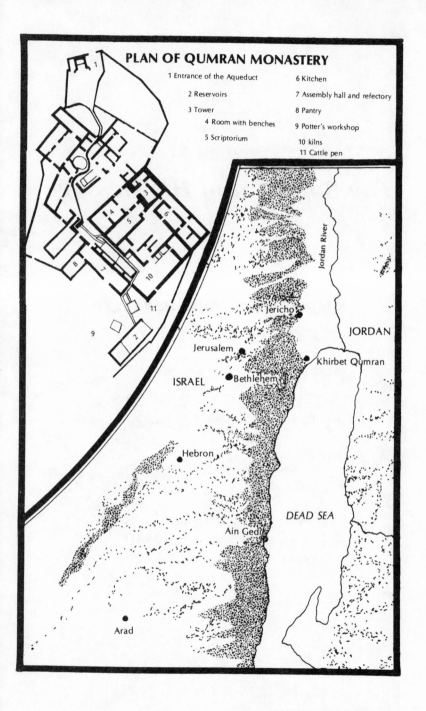

# PLAN OF QUMRAN MONASTERY

1 Entrance of the Aqueduct

2 Reservoirs

3 Tower

4 Room with benches

5 Scriptorium

6 Kitchen

7 Assembly hall and refectory

8 Pantry

9 Potter's workshop

10 kilns

11 Cattle pen

The Gospels indicate to us that John the Baptist probably provided the most immediate influence on the teaching of Jesus and so provided the immediate preparation for the coming of Jesus into public life. As is the case with Jesus himself, however, it is also the case that the Gospels do not give us a direct biography of John. Some of what they tell us is obviously reinterpreted in the hindsight of Jesus' career and resurrection, mostly to have John function as a source of Christian theology. Such would be the case, for example, where John points to Jesus with a number of salvific titles such as Lamb of God. It would also be the case where John goes out of his way to efface himself and to point to Jesus.

Using our customary principles of establishing historicity we can nevertheless draw a portrait of John as we will of Jesus. Once again the infancy narratives of the Gospels are not helpful since they are concerned with a theological presentation of John rather than biography. At best we can reasonably conclude that John was born of Zechariah and Elizabeth and was thus born into the rural and lower echelons of the priestly families. It does not seem that he was actually related to Jesus, as Luke says. That tradition was probably added to give Jesus some heritage in the priestly line. Other details of John's early years are unknown, though we may presume that he had a strict upbringing initially in the priestly circles.

When John appears on the scene in the Gospels as a young preacher he gives indication that his training did not continue exclusively in the priestly circles. He seems to reflect more the influence of the sectarians such as the Essenes at Qumran. With these sects he shares a predilection for the wilderness, a stress on apocalyptic expectations and a use of baptism for repentance. John appears in the wilderness of the Jordan River just north of the Dead Sea and not far from Jericho. In such a location he had at least to have known the Essenes at Qumran. Some would see an immediate influence, such as John's having spent years of training at the monastery. While this is problematic we must admit at least some indirect influence of sectarian movements on John.

The wilderness had in itself apocalyptic symbolism. The Jews reckoned that if God first delivered Israel by leading her through the desert, then he would again make the desert the place of final deliverance. It was undoubtedly for this reason that the Essenes established their monastery at Qumran by the Dead Sea. John would share this symbol of the final time of God's salvation even though he would not share all the apocalyptic designs of Qumran. John, for instance, did not want to restrict the final times to the select few of the monastery, and he preached openly to the crowds. Nor was he concerned with describing how the final times would come or what they would look like.

He proposed no reading of signs and portents to date the final arrival of God's judgment.

For John, however, the apocalyptic expectations were central, and we can describe John's career as preaching explicitly that the kingdom of God was imminent. John is the one to use the phrase "kingdom of God" with a frequency that was not known in the Old Testament times. The expression was recognized in the entire course of Israel's history, but John brought it to the fore as a way of summing up all that Israel expected God to do in the final time of deliverance. It is John who probably influenced Jesus to use the phrase, though Jesus gave further dimensions of meaning to it. John, as we said, did not give details of that kingdom, but simply announced that it was coming shortly. Moreover, he put stress on the negative element of the kingdom, i.e., that it would bring judgment upon those who were sinners and did not conform to God's will known through the law of Israel.

We can see how much John moved away from the mainstream of Judaism and even differentiated himself from some of the more radical elements within the religion. His preaching of final retribution would have split him from his Saducean and priestly ties, as would his asceticism and his expectations of a final kingdom that could be politically counter to the status quo of Jerusalem. While John would find some sympathy with the Pharisees who saw coming judgment on sinners, he would have alienated them because of his indifference to legalistic concerns and casuistry of the law. John would have differed from the Zealots who also expected the kingdom in that his view of the coming kingdom was not violent and anarchic to the political order. John built much on his heritage, but he moved in new directions as well.

One of the ways John especially preached about the kingdom was by proclaiming the imminent arrival of "the coming one." This was a general proclamation to embrace the varied messianic expectations of the Jews. As Israel looked forward to final redemption she sometimes pictured the coming of a messianic king like David who would establish a new political order. Other groups such as those at Qumran also anticipated a priestly messianic figure like Aaron. Still other groups with apocalyptic expectation anticipated a transcendent figure bringing an other-worldly kingdom. Such a figure would be like the Son of Man described in Daniel 7, who is given the kingdom and rules over the beasts of evil in the last days.

John seems to have expected a Messiah who would have these apocalyptic and transcendent qualities and yet would also be human. For John says on the one hand that the coming one will bring "fire and the spirit" (Mt 3:11), i.e., apocalyptic judgment and purification and re-creation. He also says on the other hand that the coming one can be compared to him in a human way, though this coming figure is mightier. Perhaps John's expectations can best be explained by saying that John probably expected a human being who would eventually be exalted and would bring an other-worldly kingdom. In any case, John's message is designed to embrace all the expectations. He took no sides in determining who was coming, but summed up any expectation by calling the figure "the coming one." For John the final time was imminent, whatever it looked like. What was even more important was not trying to picture it, but rather making a suitable response to whatever it would end up being.

Thus, for the Baptist, the preaching of the imminent kingdom led to preaching about repentance. This again is a familiar Old Testament theme, but John gave it a new urgency. Repentance means "turning around." It means moving from a life of sin to a life of justice. It means moving from one's own designs about how to run life and how to achieve one's destiny to conformity to God's will. This was a frequent message of the prophets. John had to apply it to a new situation. Some Pharisees had hardened their moral response into legalism. Even radical Qumran had petrified itself in communal discipline and rigidity. All were judging others as sinners, with their own sense of self-righteousness. John had to call everyone to a new inner response of the heart, so that there would be forgiveness in the imminent coming of the kingdom, and people would escape the coming judgment.

John was especially concerned about self-righteousness. He told the Pharisees and the Sadducees that they should not presume on the fact of their being children of Abraham: "You brood of vipers! Who warned you to flee from the wrath to come? Bear fruit that befits repentance, and do not presume to say to yourselves, 'We have Abraham as our father'; for I tell you, God is able from these stones to raise up children to Abraham" (Mt 3:7–9). The Jewish leaders were putting more on privilege than on responsibility. They assumed that being descendants of Abraham was like being on solid rock. God could not abandon them. John said that God had no absolute need for them. If they did not back up their Jewish heritage by inner righteousness and sincere repentance, then God could easily raise up a new people elsewhere.

It does not seem that John intended to say that now the covenant would embrace the Gentiles. That would be part of Jesus' new insight. John remained with his Jewish roots, but acted like the prophets in calling his people to inner response to their vocation as the people of God. Now it was even more important because the final judgment and final destiny of the people were imminent.

Central to John's exhortation to Israel was his baptism of repentance. Judaism knew of ritual washings throughout her history, and such purifications increased in the era of John and Jesus. Yet the baptism of John seems more than simply a ritual purification. If that had been all it was, there would have been nothing special about what John did. It seems more likely that John's baptism was borrowed from the sectarian movements which infused the rite with apocalyptic symbolism and initiation into the community of the last days.

In this context the baptism symbolized cleansing in moral and spiritual terms, rather than just external purification in a legal sense. The prophets often spoke of the final times as the era in which God would wash away sin. "I will sprinkle clean water upon you, and you shall be clean from all your uncleannesses, and from all your idols I will cleanse you" (Ez 36:25). The sectarians like the Essenes underwent baptism to express their hope that they would be part of the cleansed final community saved from judgment.

The baptism also served as an initiation rite into the community which considered itself the destined recipient of that final salvation. Qumran, for example, considered itself that community of the final times which would eventually know forgiveness of sins and would live the new covenant of perfect redemption. Baptism was an initiation which anticipated final cleansing and indicated that the recipient had made an act of true moral repentance and a decision to prepare for the forgiveness which God promised in the future.

John's baptism was associated then with true moral

conversion and symbolized a person's hope that God would forgive him or her at the "coming one's" judgment. It was a decision that affected one's life, so that the ritual was not repeated over and over as for ritual purifications. Moreover, the baptism did not put one into a sect, but did initiate one into an eschatological community in the wider sense. John did not gather disciples around him to isolate a new community. He sent those baptized back to their daily lives for the most part. Yet he did want them to feel part of the community of the final days, those who by sincere repentance, symbolized by baptism, were ready to face the judgment and obtain final forgiveness of sins.

Because the repentance was interior and the baptism a sign of moral "turning around," John also insisted that the repentance be followed up and continued by a religious life. In this regard John remained very much in his Jewish traditions, for he saw righteousness as keeping the Torah or law. In Luke 3:10–14, for instance, we have suggestions which, though not perhaps historically from John, would nevertheless be indicative of the kind of counsel he would give. They are examples of Jewish almsgiving in the spirit of the law, and of living well one's day-to-day Jewish life. John insisted on the internal spirit of the law, but the law was still important as such. It would be Jesus who would carry the teaching a bit farther.

Jesus came on the scene and began his public life during the preaching of John. In fact, from John Jesus most likely learned or at least had reinforced the seed thoughts that would move him beyond the orthodoxy of his day. From John he heard of dissatisfaction with the mainstream Judaism as it was practiced. He experienced apocalyptic expectations and the need for a decision that turned one toward God and his designs. He saw the need for righteous living and dedication to God's service. He appreciated the need to reach out to sinners and to avoid self-righteousness. Jesus encountered John perhaps because he had heard about John and went down from Galilee to listen to him. (Other Galileans like Simon and Andrew also did, as John 1:40 indicates.) Otherwise, perhaps Jesus was on his way to Jerusalem by way of the outer route around Samaria and met John in his travels.

In any case Jesus was baptized by John to associate himself with those who sought to prepare for the imminent kingdom. In all probability John did not yet know of Jesus and what would be his preaching. The fact that later on in prison John would send disciples to inquire if Jesus were truly "the coming one" indicates that the question was dawning on him only late in his career.

John did consider himself the one preparing for the one who was to come, but he did not know that person or how he was coming. John simply saw himself as the one described in later prophetic writing and in traditions that developed after the Old Testament just before his own time. At the end of the Old Testament history prophecy ceased for Israel and she developed the belief that the resurgence of prophecy would come only in the final times of salvation (cf. Jl 2:28). As tradition developed, Judaism expected that when the final times arrived it would be heralded not by many prophets but by *a* prophet or *the* prophet. Some considered him to be Elijah returned, others Moses, others did not name him at all. Later Jesus will consider John Elijah returned (Mk 9:11–13), but John himself was probably vague as to the name. What John was convinced of was that he had the role of *the* prophet heralding the imminent coming of the kingdom.

Jesus probably stayed with John for a short while. Although John did not have a sect, he did allow a small group of disciples to help him and to hear his teaching.

The Synoptic Gospels give the impression that Jesus left John immediately after his baptism and never had contact again. The Gospel of John is probably more accurate in this regard, saying that Jesus did associate with John for a short while. Then Jesus probably gathered his first disciples from among John's and set off to continue the same kind of preaching as John. They had overlapping ministries for a time, with Jesus in Judea and John farther up the Jordan in Samaria (Jn 3:22–24).

Gradually, however, the groups split. John 4:1–3 hints that it was because Jesus had greater success and gathered more disciples. It was probably also because Jesus began to diverge in his teaching. At this point Jesus went to Galilee and began the first major part of his intensive preaching career as recorded in the Synoptic Gospels. There does not seem to have been any bitterness in the split between Jesus and John. This is indicated by the fact that John did send disciples when he was in prison to ask Jesus if he was the one to come, and also by the fact that John's disciples came to tell Jesus when John was beheaded in prison by Herod Antipas because of John's moral indictment of the king.

The parting of the ways was inevitable since Jesus had a unique message that was gradually developing beyond his Jewish roots. He had learned much from John but there were significant differences which we will see in the coming chapters. To note them briefly now: John was ascetic, Jesus less so. John remained in the desert and had people come to him; Jesus moved to the people, even to the homes of sinners. John was stern and stressed judgment; Jesus was more optimistic and preached good news. John saw the kingdom as future though imminent; Jesus saw the kingdom as future but also saw it as partially present. John worked no signs; Jesus did. John gave central place to the law; Jesus went beyond it. John remained Jewish in his teaching; Jesus moved to a more universal message. John left the impression of earning the kingdom by repentance; Jesus emphasized it as pure gift.


## *Suggestions for Additional Reading:*

Scobie, Charles H.H. *John the Baptist.* Fortress, 1964.

Kraeling, Carl H. *John the Baptist.* Charles Scribner's Sons, 1951.

Steinmann, Jean. *Saint John the Baptist and the Desert Tradition.* Harper and Brothers, 1958.

# Jesus the Teacher

## Suggested Scripture Readings:

| Matthew | Mark |
|---------|------|
| 12:38–42 | 1:14–15; 21–28 |
| | 8:27–30 |
| | 10:13–31 |

| Luke | John |
|------|------|
| 8:1–3 | 1:35–39 |
| 10:38–42 | |

# A Rabbinic Parable
*(Compare with Matthew 22:1–14)*

R. Judah ha-Nasi said: To what may this be likened? To a king who made a banquet to which he invited guests. He said to them, 'Go, wash yourselves, brush up your clothes, anoint yourselves with oil, wash your garments, and prepare yourselves for the banquet,' but he fixed no time when they were to come to it. The wise among them walked about by the entrance of the king's palace, saying, 'Does the king's palace lack anything?' The foolish among them paid no regard or attention to the king's command. They said, 'We will in due course notice when the king's banquet is to take place, because can there be a banquet without labour [to prepare it] and company?' So the plasterer went to his plaster, the potter to his clay, the smith to his charcoal, the washer to his laundry. Suddenly the king ordered, 'Let them all come to the banquet.' They hurried the guests, so that some came in their splendid attire and others came in their dirty garments. The king was pleased with the wise ones who had obeyed his command, and also because they had shown honour to the king's palace. He was angry with the fools who had neglected his command and disgraced his palace. The king said, 'Let those who have prepared themselves for the banquet come and eat of the king's meal, but those who have not prepared themselves shall not partake of it.' You might suppose that the latter were simply to depart; but the king continued, 'No, [they are not to depart]; but the former shall recline and eat and drink, while these shall remain standing, be punished, and look on and be grieved.'

——Commentary on Ecclesiastes 9:8
"Let thy garments be always white;
and let thy head lack no oil."

As Jesus emerged into his own with a career in Galilee he began to elicit recognition from the people. In some ways the recognition was customary and expected for that time. In other ways it was unique. The diverse reactions corresponded in many ways to the manner in which Jesus was and was not like the rabbis the people knew. There seems little doubt that Jesus emerged very much in a rabbinic role. The people certainly acknowledged him as "Rabbi," though they probably had little choice but to fall into some customary title when confronted by Jesus' religious leadership.

Nevertheless, the title seems accurate in large part. The rabbis devoted themselves a great deal to the interpretation of the Scriptures. We have already spoken of Jesus' training in the sacred writings, and we see evidence of his citation of biblical texts in the manner of the rabbis: "Have you not read?" (Mt 12:3-5); "How is it written?" (Lk 10:26). Jesus also preached in the synagogues and on the sabbath, and he gathered disciples around him as did the scribes or rabbis of his day. He taught his followers by assuming their Old Testament knowledge and by at least starting with the authority of the law. "Is it lawful for a man to divorce his wife?" was a question raised by the Pharisees. Jesus answered, "What did Moses command you?" (Mk 10:2–9). When the rich young man asked Jesus what to do for perfection, Jesus began by telling him he knew the commandments.

Often Jesus himself would begin with questions and would lead disciples and opponents into biblical interpretation by way of the ensuing discussion (Mk 12:35–37). More often he used parables. These stories were designed to invite people to pass judgment on the fictitious situation and then to find for themselves the implications and the challenge for actual life. The parable of the guest without a wedding garment is a story with parallels in rabbinic literature. Though Jesus probably drew a different implication from the story it shows how close he was to rabbinic style.

Some of the parables used by Jesus employed the rabbinic method of a fortiori argumentation. Jesus showed, for instance, that if an unjust judge would eventually hear the case of an oppressed widow, "how much more" would God hear the case of an afflicted person (Lk 18:1–8). He pointed out that if a father would not give a serpent but would grant the request of a son for fish, "how much more" would God hear the request of his people in prayer (Lk 11:11–13).

The parables were designed to get a message across in a simple style, easily understood, within the context of day to day living. They served that purpose even more so in the days of Jesus before they were made more complex as allegories and before they were given new meanings in the hindsight of resurrection. Confirmation of the simple and direct message of the parables comes from the other sayings that can be traced to the historical Jesus. Many of these also follow the rabbinic style and consist of vivid, pithy and incisive statements that make their point quickly and concisely.

Like the rabbis of his time Jesus needed to rely on oral tradition and on memory to retain his teaching. He employed rhetorical devices that aided memory. Such devices included short sayings that exhibited parallel structures by repeating a thought in two different ways or by stating a thought and then its opposite. We hear Jesus say, "Ask, and it will be given to you; seek, and you will find; knock, and it will be opened to you" (Lk 11:9). We also hear Jesus preach, "The sabbath was made for man, not man for the sabbath" (Mk 2:27). Jesus teased with paradoxical sayings, and with hyperboles. He coined proverbs and spoke with irony. He knew how to convey his message, and he also knew how to make it remembered.

A number of sayings of Jesus find almost exact parallels in rabbinic writing:

"Do not worry over tomorrow's cares, for you do not know what the day will bring. Perhaps you will not be alive tomorrow, and then you would have tortured yourself over matters which no longer concern you. There is enough trouble for each hour" (cf. Mt 6:34).

"A man is measured by the measure with which he measures" (cf. Mt 7:2).

"Be not like servants who serve their masters because of the need of wages. Be rather like servants who serve their masters without need of wages" (cf. Lk 17:7–10).

While the Gospels show us what it meant to be a religious teacher of that day and while they show how much Jesus could be called a scribe or rabbi, these same Gospels also show how different and unique Jesus was. For one thing Jesus used the parables much more frequently than the rabbis. In fact we can be fairly certain that the parables were the centerpiece of the preaching of the historical Jesus. Moreover, the parables were not aids to other teaching as they were for the rabbis. Among these Jewish scribes the stories were designed to help explain authoritatively prescribed texts. What was of central importance was the meaning of a biblical passage, not the story itself. For Jesus, however, the parable itself was the message. The truth he was trying to convey was contained in the story itself.

The teaching of Jesus differed from the rabbis in its ambiance and audience as well. Rather than being confined to the synagogue or rabbinic school, Jesus taught in the open fields, on the lake, during wanderings over the land. He embraced sinners and outcasts and those who were rejected by the rabbis. He included children in his embrace and was the essence of informality. Even the way in which Jesus related to his disciples was far different from the rabbis'. He was not concerned with training his followers in a long tradition, nor with training them to continue that tradition. Rabbis expected that their followers would one day become masters on their own and would continue the traditions they learned. Jesus preached in such a way that his disciples would always remain in a master-disciple relationship with him. Besides, Jesus' followers did not choose simply to follow their master. They were chosen.

There was another notable difference in the relations of Jesus to followers that contrasted him to the rabbis. This relationship involved the attitude of Jesus toward women. It is a well-known fact that women were in a subordinate position in Jewish society of that time. They were socially restricted to domestic affairs and were considered possessions of the husband. One Jewish author wrote: "The women are best suited to the indoor life which never strays from the house." Religious teaching simply confirmed the social structure. Women were not permitted into the inner courtyards of the temple and were held only to those obligations that were the slave's.

Rabbis maintained these attitudes toward women, summed up in a rabbinic proverb, "Do not speak much with a woman on the street." Jesus broke forcefully with such attitudes. Whereas the prevailing views saw women only in relation to men, Jesus saw them in their own right as persons. Whereas women were seen usually as objects of sex and childbearing, Jesus saw them as individuals with minds and talents and personalities.

A number of the healings of Jesus were of women, such as Peter's mother-in-law, the woman with the hemorrhage, and the woman with the crippling disease that kept her bent in posture. Jesus allowed himself to be influenced by women, such as the Syro-Phoenician woman who pleaded her case before Jesus in behalf of her possessed daughter. Jesus used women as the central figures in some parables, sometimes even having them symbolize God and divine action (cf. the woman searching for the lost coin as God seeks the sinner). Most impressively of all, Jesus had close friends among women, such as Martha and Mary, and even allowed a group of women to associate closely with his band of disciples. They are described as ministering to him and his followers (Lk 8:1–3). This special affection of Jesus, which differentiated him so much from the rabbis, bore special fruit in the fidelity of the women to Jesus. Among all the followers of Jesus only the women are mentioned as remaining with Jesus through to his death, and there is never a mention in the Gospels of a woman abandoning her close tie with Jesus.

Perhaps the most noticeable difference between Jesus and the rabbis was in their claims to authority. The rabbis never claimed to speak on their own authority but always as interpreters of a tradition. Their authority rested on the authority of Moses and the original law. Their teaching could have validity only if it could be shown to be in conformity with the traditions. Jesus ultimately had no official sanction behind him and no ultimate authority on which he rested his own. He spoke in his own name and made claims to speak as he knew God wanted him to speak. This new claim to authority is what drew amazement from the crowds who wondered how he dared to speak with such authority.

It may be that Jesus differed somewhat from the rabbinic style also because he fit somewhat into the prophetic mold. He followed in the steps of the Baptist and his message. Such a preaching moved beyond the rabbinic concerns of a given society and acceptable mores. It broke with the mainstream of opinions and called for new things. The call to repentance showed a prophetic stance. Jesus referred to himself as a prophet on a number of occasions: "A prophet is without honor in his own country"; "No sign shall be given except the sign of the prophet Jonah ... and behold, something greater than Jonah is here." One final indication of Jesus' prophetic cast is his use of symbolic actions. Just as the prophets often conveyed their message by actions rather than words, so Jesus sometimes did the same. Most important of all his actions were the healings which he performed. They were symbolic of his message about the arrival of the final times. We will see this meaning of the healings of Jesus later, as we consider details of his message.

As for the rabbinic role, however, so also for the prophetic role can we say that Jesus showed differences as well as similarities. Jesus was unlike the Baptist in that his tone was less negative and his manner less ascetic. He called to repentance but did not dwell on judgment. Unlike any of the prophets who came before him, Jesus showed a more personal authority. He did not use the prophetic introduction, "Thus says the Lord," and we have no indication that he ever felt the call specifically to be a prophet. His call was to a different kind of relationship to God that brought a special kind of authority. Finally, as we shall see, Jesus, unlike the prophets, did not preach simply with future anticipations. His teaching was suffused with a sense of present realities.

We have dwelt on the background and the preparation of Jesus, and we have considered his style and manner of preaching. All of this leads to the main point of consideration, namely, the content of Jesus' message. It is above all in what he had to say that Jesus showed his Jewish roots and continuity with the past. It is in that same message that he showed his uniqueness. Jesus lived a long experience of poverty and associated with the poor. His preaching spoke to that situation. Jesus learned of the many expectations of religion around him. He addressed all those concerns. Jesus learned from the Baptist. He embraced John's message and moved beyond it. He took the style of the rabbis and prophets, but he added new dimensions. His sayings and parables and his healings converged on a message both new and old. We can sum it all up in one grand theme that formed the center of the preaching of the Jesus of history: "The kingdom of God is upon you."

If Jesus could say *the* kingdom of God is upon you, then it seems likely that he was referring to something within the experience of his hearers: "*The* kingdom which you are awaiting is upon you." Jesus could very well have taken the term from John the Baptist. Yet he would use it to summarize all the varied expectations of the time and would give even more dimensions to the term than John. Whereas John spent most of his time preaching the response that was the preparation for the kingdom, Jesus spent time talking of the kingdom itself.

*The* kingdom that some of the Jews were expecting had apocalyptic overtones. Certainly the Zealots and most likely some of the Pharisees awaited an other-worldly and future achievement of God's final redemption. Evil was seen as so entrenched in our world that it could only be overcome by God's action and by a transformation of our creation beyond history as we know it. Jesus embraced this transcendent view of the kingdom and seems also to have awaited an imminent arrival of an other-worldly kingdom: "There are some of those standing here who will not taste of death until they have seen that the kingdom of God has come with power" (Mk 9:1).

Nevertheless, Jesus did not accept the Zealot view of doing violence in order to bring in the kingdom. Nor did he think, as others did, that one could anticipate or predict the coming of the kingdom by signs and portents. Jesus took from the apocalyptic view the conviction that the kingdom would have to be God's work and that it would ultimately be a transcendent other-worldly reality. Exactly when it would arrive and what it would look like he did not speculate about.

Paradoxically, while Jesus knew of an apocalyptic kingdom, he also spoke of another aspect of the kingdom which would be present in this world reality. He urged his disciples to pray, "Your kingdom come on earth as it is in heaven." This was a return to the future expectations of the prophets who were concerned with this world reality and a final salvation from God that would affect this history and this world reality. It was a current of thought in the Palestine of Jesus' time.

What *the* this-worldly kingdom would look like gave itself to divergent pictures. There were some of the separatists among the Pharisees and others, no doubt, who anticipated a political kingdom with another Davidic king messiah who would establish an independent Israel once again. Jesus did not envision the imminent kingdom as a political empire. It is for that reason more than any other that we find the strange fact that Jesus never claimed to be Messiah in his lifetime. Since he would be misunderstood, he did not use the title Messiah and chose instead titles like Son of Man which would not bear political overtones. It is only after the resurrection that the title Messiah will be given to Jesus, and it is not a title that belongs to the Jesus of history.

To say that the kingdom is not a political kingdom is not to say that it has no political implications. We shall see that some of the unique aspects of Jesus' teaching put a heavy emphasis on the poor and the outcasts. This had profound meaning for the social structures of society which could be indicted for indifference or for oppression of the poor. Thus, for the historical Jesus it is fair to say that while there was not a political kingdom there was such a thing as kingdom politics. The future kingdom that was coming would have an effect on the social and political structures of this world and this history.

For Jesus also *the* kingdom seemed not to be just for external social structures. It was an internal, spiritual reality as well, calling for a change of heart. In this way the preaching of Jesus embraced those Pharisees and others who envisioned the kingdom as a future reality to be anticipated in quiet obedience to the law, with patience and humility. "Seek first his kingdom and his righteousness and all these things (food, clothing, etc.) shall be yours as well" (Mt 6:33). We shall see, of course, that Jesus had differing views as to the ultimate meaning of the law, but he was not opposed to the Jewish views of his time that saw the kingdom as a spiritual reality calling for inner virtue.

As we gather up all these insights into the kingdom we see how much Jesus built on his Jewish roots. In actuality Jesus did not accept just one school of thought and totally dismiss the others. Nor did he simply adhere to any complete Jewish viewpoint. His preaching said in effect that everyone had a part of the truth, but he brought each piece into a new configuration so that the end result was a unique and surprising proclamation. *The* kingdom of God was indeed other-worldly, but it also had an effect on this-world reality. It was a spiritual kingdom but could not be restricted to just inward and individual concerns. It had social and political ramifications even if it could not be described directly as a political kingdom. It would have revolutionary implications, but would not be violent.

Jesus had, in effect, declared that everyone was right and everyone was wrong. This would have been enough in itself to create hostility with the orthodoxy of his day and even with the sectarianism of the times. It was already a unique kind of message. Yet Jesus added two further elements that would carry him beyond his Jewish roots and would lead him to a totally unique message about the final time of salvation. Judaism, in all of its varied expectations of the kingdom, was always looking to a future point. Even if some saw the kingdom as imminent, it was still a future reality. Jesus made a new step when he declared that the kingdom was not only future, but was a present reality beginning now.

According to Jesus, God had indeed begun his work of the final inbreaking into history. Ultimate redemption would require a future and final transcendent event, but God was beginning that work mysteriously in the present and in this world reality. One could not necessarily see the full effects of this present work of the kingdom, but it was taking shape in the preaching and activity of Jesus himself. It called for new relationships, new motivation, new reasons for repentance.

Much of the Judaism of Jesus' time limited the idea of the kingdom to Israel herself, and some restricted it even to certain Israelites. Jesus moved in the other direction, opening the kingdom to a universal audience. This again gave him a unique message and one designed to create friction with his people.

With this preaching of the kingdom Jesus launched his full public career. We have now to explore in more detail especially the unique aspects of that preaching and to draw the full implications of what it meant to proclaim a kingdom that was present now, and a kingdom that embraced all people.

## *Suggestions for Additional Reading:*

Feuillet, André. "The Reign of God and the Person of Jesus According to the Synoptic Gospels," in André Robert and André Feuillet, eds. *Introduction to the New Testament.* Desclee Co, 1965, Conclusion, Chapter 1.

Mitton, C. Leslie. *Your Kingdom Come.* Eerdmans, 1978.

Dodd, Charles H. *The Founder of Christianity.* Macmillan, 1970.

Bornkamm, Günther. *Jesus of Nazareth.* Harper, 1960. (A major study, but a bit more scholarly in tone.)

Brown, Raymond. *Jesus: God and Man.* Bruce, 1967.

# A New Message

## Suggested Scripture Readings:

| Matthew | Mark |
|---------|------|
| 5:1–48 | 2:15–17 |
| 8:5–13 | |
| 11:1–30 | |
| 13:1–51 | |
| 18:1–35 | |

### Luke

4:16–21
11:14–26

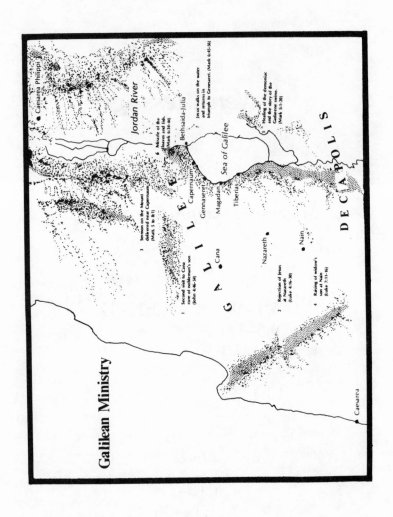

Galilean Ministry

Caesarea Philippi

Jordan River

6 Miracle of the
loaves and fish.
(Mark 6:34-44)

Bethsaida-Julias

7 Jesus walks on the water
and returns in
triumph to Gennesaret. (Mark 6:45-56)

5 Healing of the demoniac
and the entry of the
Gadarene swine.
(Mark 5:1-20)

Capernaum

Sea of Galilee

Gennesaret

Magadan

Tiberias

G A L I L E E

3 Sermon on the Mount
delivered near Capernaum
(Matt. 5 to 8:1)

1 Second visit to Cana
cure of nobleman's son
(John 4:46-54)

Cana

Nazareth

Nain

2 Rejection of Jesus
at Nazareth
(Luke 4:16-30)

4 Raising of widow's
son at Nain
(Luke 7:11-16)

D E C A P O L I S

Caesarea

From at least the time of his baptism by John, and his being influenced by this man whom he himself described as "the greatest of men, more than a prophet," Jesus sensed the uniqueness of his mission from the Father. He learned from John the call to repentance by which he would summon people. He learned also to go beyond nationalism or self-righteousness, and he gave a more universal message of salvation, at least to the point of accepting sinners and the outcasts of society. Yet Jesus seemed to sense an even greater role for himself.

Whereas John remained in his Jewish roots, gathering a people who would be prepared for a coming final time of salvation, Jesus felt and preached that the final times were already beginning. Hence, while John called to repentance *in order to* enter the coming kingdom, Jesus called to repentance *as a result of* the kingdom which was already dawning. "I solemnly assure you, history has not known a man born of woman greater than John the Bap-

tizer. Yet the least born into the kingdom of God is greater than he" (Mt 11:11).

This new message which Jesus carried on, in part
from the Baptist, and in part from his own unique insight,
took more and more definite shape with the development
of Jesus' public life. As he gathered his disciples he distin-
guished from among them a group designated as the
twelve. It was a symbolic gesture, representing a replace-
ment of the twelve tribes and pointing to the new Israel,
the community of the final days of salvation now unfolding. All that Jesus did and spoke pointed to the kingdom
as the central point of his proclamation. If the Baptist had
already met opposition from the religious leaders of his
day because of his innovative call to sinners to repent for
an imminent kingdom, it was only inevitable that Jesus
would rattle orthodoxy by completing the message.

Various teachings became explicit as Jesus proclaimed
the inbreaking of the kingdom. Let us examine each aspect
which came to diverge from the teachings of Judaism
around him. Religious leaders would begin to notice a
new message as they accumulated the new phrases and ex-
pressions that Jesus coined: "The kingdom of God suffers
violence; enter the kingdom of God; the least in the kingdom of God; the kingdom prepared; to inherit the kingdom; not to be far from the kingdom; the kingdom of
heaven is like . . ." The startling, creative and innovative
point of the preaching came over and over: the kingdom
was already dawning and the time of God's grace was *today.*

Some of the parables uttered by Jesus were intended
to stress this point, although they seem to have acquired
another interpretation as they appear now in the Gospels.
For example, the parable of the sower, as used by Jesus,
was designed to put the emphasis in the story on the pow-

er of the seed. We tend to use the parable as an allegory with stress on the soil. We give meaning to each place where the seed falls.

As Jesus used the parable it implied that the kingdom was already being accomplished even if it did not seem so in the life of Jesus. Just as the seed thrown by the farmer seemed to be scattered uselessly and without results, so the life of Jesus seemed to be achieving nothing. Nevertheless, the seed sooner or later reached good soil and produced fruit. So, too, the life of Jesus was bearing fruit, for the kingdom was secretly working already in his lifetime.

As Jesus used the parable of the treasure in the field or the pearl of great price, he was not referring to the kingdom as a precious object to be found at the end of time. One did not sell all one had to acquire a prize in the future and in another world. Rather, the treasure and the pearl represented present realities to be sought immediately and wholeheartedly. The kingdom was already there in its secret workings, to be uncovered.

That the orthodoxy of his day did not yet envision the kingdom as present is seen from some of the dialogue of Jesus with the Jewish leaders. These religious men had their own ideas of what the kingdom would look like and how it would come. It was still a future hope to be awaited. Then Jesus came on the scene with a new message. "Once, on being asked by the Pharisees when the reign of God would come, he replied: 'You cannot tell by careful watching when the reign of God will come. Neither is it a matter of reporting that it is "here" or "there." The reign of God is already in your midst' " (Lk 17:20–21).

The healing miracles of Jesus were showing in deed what he was proclaiming in word. We cannot easily reconstruct what actually happened in the history of Jesus. The miracle stories have been reworked and enlarged to proclaim a fuller theology of Jesus in the hindsight of the resurrection. Many of the stories that we have may be theologically symbolic stories rather than biography. Nevertheless, it seems a solid fact of history that Jesus did perform some miracles. Scholars are more skeptical of the nature miracles, such as the wine miracle of Cana, or of stories such as the raising of Lazarus. There seems more historicity behind the healings of Jesus. We may not be able to ascertain which miracles are authentic, and we do have a sense that all of them are reworked. We can, however, be reasonably sure that all the healings *in globo* witness to the fact of miracles in the life of Jesus.

One story especially points to the historicity of healings. The enemies of Jesus on one occasion accused him of casting out demons by the power of the prince of demons. They spoke of healings in their mentality, which saw healings as exorcisms. Still, they admitted that Jesus healed. They could not deny the basic fact, but only the meaning of the healings. The accusation also enabled Jesus to interpret the meaning of the deeds. They pointed to the kingdom's presence, a witness that moved Jesus again away from the orthodoxy of his day: "If Satan is expelling Satan, he must be torn by dissension. How, then, can his dominion last? . . . But if it is by the Spirit of God that I expel demons, then the reign of God has overtaken you" (Mt 12:26–28).

It may be that some of the acts of Jesus were simple acts of human compassion which then became dramatized as miracles or exorcisms. It may be that some of the healings were more dramatic in their actual occurrence. In both cases they were prophetic symbolism. The kingdom was God's breaking into our history. It was God transforming our creation by the conquering of all evil. If that kind of kingdom was truly present, then Jesus had to show it and not just say it. The healings backed up his words. They showed God as already beginning the transformation of this world. They were manifestations in action that the kingdom was already present.

Such an interpretation does not have to point to the divinity of Jesus. Many people over the course of history have been instruments of God's miracles without being divine. Even as Jesus performed healings he did so not to make claims about himself, but to point to the work of the kingdom which the Father was doing through him. Later insight after the resurrection would recognize the divinity of Jesus as a faith commitment and would infuse this element as part of the miracle stories. The Jesus of history made simpler claims, i.e., that the kingdom which had still to come with all its achievement in the near future was at least making a start in his deeds as well as in his words.

The present reality of the kingdom put humanity into a new relationship with God, and Jesus once again moved from the traditional views of his day to a new and deeper vision of God. In his own prayers, in the prayer which he taught his disciples, in his preaching, Jesus called God "Father." The Aramaic expression he used was "Abba," a term of intimacy and affection, closer to the meaning "Dad" than to "Father." It was an intimate word which bespeaks confidence and security. Nowhere in the Old Testament is God addressed as Father in the context of prayer, and even outside of prayer the title is usually avoided because it was used in everyday talk as a word of familiarity. It must have been startling to hear the man Jesus always address God in this way, yet that was the heart of his new message. God had, as a matter of fact, come to humanity with a new kingdom and was showing himself through Jesus as "Dad."

If the kingly rule of God brought him as Abba, then it also established humanity as children of God. Another central point of the new message of Jesus was his insistence: "I assure you, unless you change and become like little children, you will not enter the kingdom of God" (Mt 18:3). Jesus was not telling people they must be innocent or naive. Nor was he assuming a relationship that was sentimental and weak. Rather, he was emphasizing a relationship of genuine dependence and trust. God truly was close to humanity, God was bringing his kingdom, but humanity had to open itself to God's work and will.

Many Jews of the time saw salvation as humanity's work and merit. Jesus preached the kingdom as God's work. Humanity needs to stand before the Father in utter confidence, even in suffering and mystery, that God knows what he is doing. "It is no part of your heavenly Father's plan that a single one of these little ones shall ever come to grief" (Mt 18:14); "I offer you praise, O Father, Lord of heaven and earth, because what you have hidden from the learned and the clever you have revealed to the merest children" (Lk 10:21); "Do not live in fear, little flock. It has pleased your Father to give you the kingdom" (Lk 12:32).

It is in this context that Christ preached a new message of repentance. For Israel this process was much more an act of self-effacement and an effort at human self-mastery. It was regret at the past and good solid effort to improve in the future. The Pharisees saw one as the object of God's love only after one had proved earnestness in repentance by good deeds. Jesus showed repentance to be much more a change of heart than a change of actions; he made it an obligation for all and not just for the outcasts of society. Most of all, he made it a response to God's forgiving grace rather than its prerequisite. Jesus preached the first step of repentance as affirmation of one's guilt. Like the younger son in the parable of the prodigal son, or like the publican in the parable of the Pharisee and the publican, one must acknowledge: "I am a sinner."

Yet repentance means more than just being sorry. It leads to a turning away from sin, and a wholehearted turning at that. "When the unclean spirit departs from a man, it roams through arid wastes searching for a place of rest and finding none. Then it says, 'I will go back where I came from,' and returns to find the dwelling unoccupied, though swept and tidied now. Off it goes again to bring back with it this time seven spirits more evil than itself" (Mt 12:43–45). Jesus is not speaking of inevitable consequences, but of half-hearted conversion. The dwelling was swept and tidied, but not occupied by a new master. Repentance was half-heartedly begun, but not a total turning to the Father.

Even more than these points the preaching of Jesus put repentance beyond this process of being sorry and even of complete surrender to a new master. It was precisely at this point that his call had a new ring to it. His surrender was not primarily in reformed actions, good deeds, works of merit. It consisted chiefly in a change of heart. "Unless you change and become like little children . . ." (Mt 18:3). Genuine repentance means being able to say "Abba" once again, to put one's trust in the Father, to find one's way home again as the prodigal son toward his Father's arms.

Finally, Jesus took one beyond the traditions of his day and even beyond the Baptist's call to true repentance by making it a response to God's initiative. Jesus calls Zacchaeus, and his invitation brings the tax collector to repent. Jesus forgives the sinful woman, and that brings her to love and repentance. In the parable of the two debtors

Jesus shows that the one who is more grateful is the one to whom the larger sum is remitted. God loves first. The kingdom is present already; *therefore,* repentance is called for.

As sharply as all this teaching and activity of Jesus diverged from the Judaism of his day, nothing seemed so startling as his overtures to the sinners and the outcasts of society. On the one hand, it reminded even the religious leaders that they had need of repentance, simply because all people need to be called to childlike trust and dependence. On the other hand, it strengthened the point of the Father's initiative, because even those who seemed the farthest from him were in fact brought close by his invitation.

In the Old Testament Israel's prophets already had instilled a concept of the coming kingdom as the end of all sorrow, suffering and imperfection. Isaiah spoke of a coming servant who would be anointed by the Spirit to bring good tidings to the poor, to bind up the brokenhearted, to proclaim liberty to captives. He saw a time when the eyes of the blind would be opened and the ears of the deaf unstopped. The kingdom would bring the consummation of the world and the fullness of gifts.

By the time of Jesus these gifts were seen by many as remote expectations in the future, so that they had little bearing on the immediate practices of Judaism. The prominent thought of many was, as we have seen, the restoration of Israel as a nation. To this national particularism could be added what we have said about the Pharisees' stressing human merit of the kingdom over God's initiative. It led to further discrimination within Israel itself. The one seen as deserving of the Lord's favor was the one who kept the laws, who abided by Jewish practices, who was deemed truly righteous. The unfortunate of society were considered by their very misfortune to be sinners. They were to be shunned because one was especially to avoid contamination from the unrighteous. Separatism on all counts was the basic trend.

How unorthodox Jesus must have seemed when he said he came for the sinners and for the poor! When he proclaimed the kingdom as already present in some way, he heralded the completion of all the expectations of the prophets like Isaiah. He went into the synagogue in Nazareth, read the scroll of Isaiah which proclaimed the fullness of gifts when the kingdom would come, and then declared: "Today this Scripture passage is fulfilled in your hearing" (Lk 4:21). Jesus declared: "The Spirit of the Lord is upon me . . . to bring glad tidings to the poor, to proclaim liberty to captives, recovery of sight to the blind and release to prisoners" (Lk 4:18).

On another occasion, when John the Baptist sent his disciples to Jesus to inquire whether he was "the coming one," Jesus gave signs that he was indeed the one to announce the arrival of the kingdom. The signs Jesus offered were in his reaching out to the poor and the outcasts of society: "Go back and report to John what you hear and see: the blind recover their sight, cripples walk, lepers are cured, the deaf hear, dead men are raised to life, and the poor have the good news preached to them" (Mt 11:4–6). Jesus knew that this would upset the orthodoxy of his time, for he added, "Blest is the man who finds no stumbling block in me."

It seems that Jesus himself restricted his own preaching to Israel, but his central concern for the poor and the sinners had an open perspective quite contrary to many of the religious leaders of his times. He himself said, "My mission is only to the lost sheep of the house of Israel" (Mt 15:24), and he himself sent disciples in his lifetime only to the lost sheep of the house of Israel. Nevertheless, when Gentiles approached him, he did not reject them, as is seen in his healings of the children of the Roman centurion and the Syro-Phoenician woman. Christ also had a sense that eventually his message would go to all people, perhaps even because of the opposition from the religious traditions of his day: "Mark what I say! Many will come from the east and the west and will find a place at the banquet in the kingdom of Abraham, Isaac, and Jacob, while the natural heirs of the kingdom will be driven out into the dark" (Mt 8:11–12).

As Jesus became more and more known in his public life, the accusation brought before him was, "This man welcomes sinners and eats with them" (Lk 15:2). It led Jesus to preach a whole series of parables that challenged the religious leaders and told them that a central point of his kingdom message is the forgiveness of sins. The parable of the prodigal son contrasted the love of the Father with the disdain of the elder son, the righteous keeper of the law who had no use for the sinner. The parable of the Pharisee and the publican showed that God heard the prayer of the sinner. The story of the workers in the vineyard who came at different hours but all received the same wage stressed that God loves the eleventh hour people. The parables of the lost sheep and the lost coin make it perfectly clear that "there will be more joy in heaven over one repentant sinner than over ninety-nine righteous people who have no need to repent" (Lk 15:7).

In reality, as Jesus taught that he came for the poor and the sinners, he was indicting the religious leaders. He was saying, in effect, that their so-called righteousness was really keeping them remote from God, and that they needed to change their hearts and to turn from self-reliance to trust in God and his work of the kingdom. The parable of the two sons exposed the facts. Some people say that they will do the Father's will, but don't; others say they will not do the Father's will, but end up doing it. Likewise, the religious leaders are like those who find excuses for not coming when a man gives a banquet. They have all kinds of things that they consider important in their own eyes, yet they are really refusing the call to the kingdom. They trust themselves and their pious practices, but do not trust the Lord and his work. Jesus declared: "Tax collectors and prostitutes are entering the kingdom of God before you" (Mt 21:31).

Of course, Old Testament law, the Torah, had originally been intended to foster inner attitudes and a trust relationship to God. Moreover, it contained within it even the exalted command to love one's neighbor. The self-righteousness of the times, however, thought less of response to what God was doing and saw the law more as an end in itself. It became an objective of human enterprise and accomplishment. Even worse, it left concern for others as less important. The command to love was simply one of many, and it had less value than hundreds of external legal prescriptions.

Jesus restored the primitive purpose of the Torah and deepened its meaning. He showed, first of all, that God takes the initiative, and humanity responds. In the parables he downplayed human merit and stressed love of others for its own sake and for the Lord's sake. The people in the parable of the last judgment are totally surprised to receive a reward for giving a cup of water to the least of the brethren. In another parable Jesus says that one does well to serve at table after working a field all day, and that after all that, one should see oneself still as an unprofitable servant. "When you have done all you have been committed to do, say, 'We are useless servants. We have done no more than our duty' " (Lk 17:10).

Jesus also deepened the Torah in making the command to love the central commandment. Moreover, the neighbor came to take on universal meaning. The parable of the good Samaritan illustrated who the neighbor was and how to be neighborly. Finally, Jesus joined the command to love neighbor to the command to love God. People were to forgive others as God forgave them, to love others as God loved them. In the parable of the merciless official, Jesus warns the hearers: "Should you not have dealt mercifully with your fellow servant, as I dealt with you?" (Mt 18:33).

In many ways the teaching of Jesus was not brand new to Israel in content. However, in practice, some of Judaism of the time of Jesus had wandered from what it knew. Jesus called it back, and then also gave new teaching that instilled a deeper motivation: the kingdom was no longer future, the day of salvation had dawned. This called for a deeper relationship to God and neighbor, and a more conscious appreciation of human motivation.

## *Suggestions for Additional Reading:*

Hunter, Archibald. *Interpreting the Parables.* Westminster, 1961.

Brown, Raymond. "The Parables of Jesus," in the *Jerome Biblical Commentary.* Prentice-Hall, 1967.

_____. "The Gospel Miracles," in the *Jerome Biblical Commentary.* Prentice-Hall, 1967.

Fuller, Reginald. *Interpreting the Miracles.* Westminster, 1963.

Jeremias, Joachim. "Abba," in *The Central Message of the New Testament*. SCM Press, 1965.

————. *New Testament Theology: The Proclamation of Jesus*. Charles Scribner's Sons, 1971. (A central study, though more specialized in tone.)

Perkins, Pheme. *Love Commands in the New Testament*. Paulist Press, 1982.

# *Jesus Against the Authorities*

## *Suggested Scripture Readings:*

| *Matthew* | *Mark* |
|-----------|--------|
| 22:1–10 | 6:1–6 |
| 23:1–39 | 11:1–33 |
| 25:1–30 | 12:13–17 |

*Luke*

11:37–54

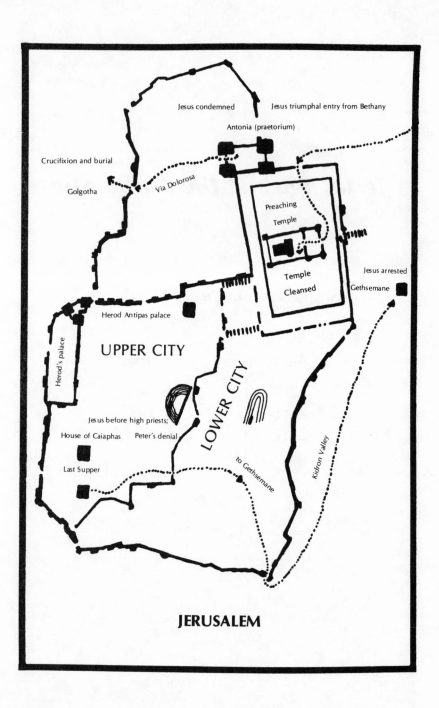

Jesus condemned

Jesus triumphal entry from Bethany

Antonia (praetorium)

Crucifixion and burial

Golgotha

Via Dolorosa

Preaching

Temple

Temple

Cleansed

Jesus arrested

Gethsemane

Herod Antipas palace

UPPER CITY

Herod's palace

LOWER CITY

Jesus before high priests;

Peter's denial

House of Caiaphas

Last Supper

to Gethsemane

Kidron Valley

JERUSALEM

From the time that Jesus took up his ministry and proclaimed the coming of the kingdom of God, his message had an urgency and an authority about it. It was bad enough that the points he emphasized were already unique to him and challenging to the orthodoxy of his time. What made matters worse was the manner of his preaching, its intensity and its earnestness. All this would make it inevitable that Jesus would come to loggerheads with many of the elements of his Jewish society, especially with its leaders.

Even from the beginning in his Galilean ministry, Jesus used numerous parables that were basically a call to decision. They were designed to provoke crisis, to have listeners evaluate their position before the Lord, and to decide then and there to turn toward the Father in complete trust and openness to the work of the kingdom that he was beginning. These parables had a sense of urgency and immediacy about them. As we have these parables today in the Gospels they have been reinterpreted in the light of the resurrection and the needs of the early Church. In some respects they have lost their punch and challenge. We do well to try to reconstruct their original meaning when used by Jesus.

This can easily be done by having the parables refer to the *first* coming of Jesus then and there, rather than to his final coming at the end of time. Jesus was asking people if they would recognize the beginnings of the kingdom in his preaching and healing, and if they would make a decision for him. When he urges his audience to beware of being caught as by a thief in the night, he is saying that in effect he has just come like a thief to surprise people with the kingdom. If they refuse conversion, then they are caught. Jesus provoked crisis and demanded immediate decision.

Adjust the audience from the faithful followers of a risen Christ to the enemies of an historical Jesus, stress the listeners as being originally the religious leaders of Israel, and you can see easily why the parables antagonized the authorities right from the start. When Jesus told the story of the people who had to develop their talents for the return of the king, he was saying that the king had just returned to seek an account from the religious leaders. He accused them of resting content with their individual talents, of settling for the current Jewish traditions and practices, of refusing to use their beliefs as a stepping stone to him and the inbreaking of the kingdom. Jesus challenged people to crisis and decision. Would they keep their talent buried or would they be good stewards open to new teaching? When this parable is seen in terms of Jesus' coming right then, and not in terms of the end of time, it bears a sense of urgency. To those who reject Jesus it also brings strong antipathy.

Many other parables gave the same challenge and

mounted up the hostility. The coming of the kingdom was like a king's giving a marriage feast. How many excuses could religious leaders find for refusing the invitation? The kingdom's arrival in the preaching of Jesus was like the arrival of the bridegroom for his wedding. How many people, especially among the leaders, would be caught as were the five foolish virgins who had no oil for their lamps?

The answers were being decided right then and there as Jesus preached. He consistently maintained a sense of urgency. It was a threat to orthodoxy. Such parables reached their culmination in the story told later in the career of Jesus. The leaders were ultimately like tenants of a vineyard who beat off the servants of the king and ultimately killed the king's son, so that they could run the vineyard according to their own desires and in their own possession. Jesus possessed the kingdom, but the religious leaders had their own ideas as to what the kingdom would be and as to who would be in it. The people in the parable said, "Here is the one who will inherit everything. Come, let us kill him, and the inheritance will be ours" (Mk 12:7).

Another characteristic of the manner of Jesus' preaching, a characteristic that was sure to antagonize religious leaders, was his unique use of the word "Amen" in his pronouncements. The word was used customarily to affirm another's words, or to ratify a prayer, an oath, a blessing or a curse. In the Gospels it is used only on the lips of Jesus, and solely to strengthen his own words. It was a statement by Jesus of his own authority. It was even stronger than the words of the prophets when they pointed to greater authority behind their statements and said, "Thus says the Lord." Jesus speaks in his own name, "Amen, Amen, I say to you." Such statements are the underlying base for the crowds to remark, "A completely new teaching in a spirit of authority!" Such statements were the only signs necessary for the authorities: "Why does this age seek a sign? Amen, Amen, I say to you, no such sign will be given it!" (Mk 8:12).

The style and self-confidence of Jesus, his sense of urgency, and the uniqueness of his message of the kingdom were all guaranteed to make his ministry less than a success story and final triumph. Even his Galilean ministry, the start of his public career, saw the gathering opposition. His healing power and his authoritative teaching seemed to draw crowds, but the dark shadows were already growing. Statements began: "Who can forgive sins except God alone?" (Mk 2:7); "Why does he eat with such as these?" (Mk 2:16); "Why does he heal on the sabbath?" (Mk 3:2).

Finally, the Galilean ministry came to a quick conclusion. Besides the accusation of the leaders that Jesus was possessed by the spirit of Beelzebul, he came also to be rejected by his relatives and townsfolk. His family thought his zeal to be simply a sign of insanity. "He is out of his mind," they charged (Mk 3:21). His fellow Nazarenes could not get past his family background. "They found him too much for them. Jesus' reply to all this was: 'No prophet is without honor except in his native place' " (Mk 6:3–4).

Forced to withdraw from the scene, Jesus began to move in the neighboring villages. While it is impossible to reconstruct the exact sequence of events, it does seem that Jesus included a brief visit to the northern pagan territories around Tyre and Sidon, and to the Gentile cities east of the Sea of Galilee. Moreover, he spent this time of partial withdrawal, not for a quiet life, nor to escape personal danger, but to regather his forces, spend time with his disciples, and prepare for the decisive mission to Jerusalem where he would make his final appeal for repentance and the kingdom, come what may! He never lost his sense of urgency. This kind of challenge would continue to irk Jewish leaders, so that the skirmishes would carry on until their culmination in Jerusalem.

Just who were the leaders affected this way by the teaching? There were, first of all, the scribes or lawyers of Israel. They were the official interpreters of the law who thus became the official teachers and theologians as well. From the very beginning tensions built between these men and Jesus. He had no formal training and was not ordained to the office, yet they called him "Rabbi," and the crowds even acknowledged that he taught with greater authority than the scribes. Very early in Jesus' career the scribes became defensive and accused Jesus of healing by the power of Beelzebul. Their reactions could only grow as he challenged their very function. In effect he told them that many did an excellent job of preaching the law, but not of living it.

Already by the Sermon on the Mount, during his Galilean ministry, Jesus said to the people, "Unless your holiness surpasses that of the scribes you shall not enter the kingdom of God" (Mt 5:20). If these learned theologians had truly lived the law, then it would have led them to a better acceptance of Jesus' preaching of the kingdom. Instead, many remained content with the letter of the law and not with its call for an inner attitude of trust and love. Jesus had to call them to that inner relationship, so he preached his famous sermon to move people from the external commands to inner attitudes: "You have heard . . . every murderer shall be liable to judgment. What I say to you is: everyone who grows angry with his brother shall be liable to judgment" (Mt 5:21–22).

When finally Jesus entered Jerusalem his battle with

the scribes came to a head. "Woe to you lawyers! You lay impossible burdens on men but you will not lift a finger to lighten them" (Lk 11:46). "Be on guard against the scribes, who like to parade around in their robes and accept marks of respect in public, front seats in the synagogues, and places of honor at banquets. . . . It is they who will receive the severest sentence" (Mk 12:38–40). Ultimately, Jesus accused them of piously calling people to atone for their fathers' killing of the prophets, while these same scribes were rejecting *the* prophet in their very midst. "Woe to you scribes! You erect tombs for the prophets. . . . You say, 'Had we lived in our forefathers' time we would not have joined them in shedding the prophets' blood.' Thus you show that you are the sons of the prophets' murderers. Now it is your turn" (Mt 23:29–32).

Many of the scribes were Pharisees, but the Pharisees were a larger group than just the scribes. Jesus found no fault with their reasons for existing, i.e., their desire for piety and for living their faith to the fullest. He even dined in the homes of Pharisees. Nevertheless, they had in-built temptations in their practices, and Jesus often challenged those who succumbed. These devout men were noted for their striving for charity, for their punctilious keeping of the hours of prayer, for weekly fasts, and for conscientious adherence to regulations for purity. Jesus must surely have antagonized them with his call to inner conversion and trust, especially when that showed up their external show, their self-righteousness, their ambition, and their hypocrisy.

The Pharisees very early wanted to know why Jesus would consort with sinners, why his disciples would pick grain on the sabbath, why Jesus would not keep all the prescriptions of the Mosaic law. Jesus would respond by his Sermon on the Mount, telling people that their holiness had to surpass that of the Pharisees as well as that of the scribes. He gave three examples from the central practices of these laymen. When you give alms, do it in secret and not in public display. When you pray, do so in private and not to be noticed by others. Do the same for fasting. It is the inner attitude that counts.

By the time Jesus reached Jerusalem, his criticisms had sharpened. "You Pharisees! You cleanse the outside of cup and dish, but within you are filled with rapaciousness and evil. . . . Woe to you Pharisees! You pay tithes on mint and rue and all the garden plants, while neglecting justice and the love of God" (Lk 11:39–42). Many Pharisees were content with following the legal prescriptions and, in fact, had developed an entire oral tradition that imposed more legal prescriptions as interpretation of the Torah. Jesus said that he was not interested in these further interpretations. He said that all the prescriptions really demanded inner purity. The Pharisees were more interested in avoiding sin than in living virtue. They were caught up in living the minor practices of piety and ignored the great moral obligations. That would give them a great sense of self-satisfaction, but it missed the meaning of the real Jewish law. When Jesus preached the arrival of the kingdom and the demands it made, he could not help but contrast with the behavior of the Pharisees. Jesus was even more radical than the radicalists of Judaism!

The last group which felt the effects of Jesus' teaching was the priests, who also belonged by and large to the movement of the Sadducees. These priests were concerned with the public worship in the temple and were socially distinct even from the rest of the priestly tribe which was scattered over the country outside of Jerusalem. They were not always concerned with the genuine meaning of the worship over which they presided, would not hesitate to cheat widows and the poor to their own advantage, and sought above all to maintain their position of authority in the capital.

Jesus had little direct contact with this group until he reached Jerusalem, it seems, but his call to trust and openness to the coming kingdom of God would breed trouble even from a distance. We do hear of Jesus sending people whom he cured to the priests to offer thanksgiving, and we do hear of Jesus telling of the priests who passed by the man felled by robbers, quite in contrast to the Samaritan who stopped. Undoubtedly Jesus' message of worship in spirit and in truth and his relativizing of the temple for the greater event of the kingdom would send the chief priests to join the scribes in attacking the authority of Jesus.

Although we are not sure, it may be historical fact that the priests eventually became the strongest opponents of Jesus, who eventually brought him to death. In John's Gospel one priest says, "Can you not see that it is better for you to have one man die than to have the whole nation destroyed?" (Jn 11:50). The other Gospels say that the priests and the scribes sought to arrest Jesus, but had to find a way to do this, because they feared his popularity among the people.

In all the leadership that we have described thus far, the focus has been on the religious authorities. It seems that this is what underlies the Gospel in its true history, and that we cannot bring the secular Roman authorities into the conflict until the actual trial of Jesus. Some have wanted to make Jesus a revolutionary eager to overthrow the Roman government that ruled in the person of the procurator. We do have also a scene where Jesus speaks against Herod Antipas of Galilee. When Pharisees sought to threaten Jesus into leaving Galilee by saying that Herod was trying to kill him, Jesus responded, "Go tell that fox, 'Today and tomorrow I cast out devils and perform cures, and on the third day my purpose is accomplished. For all that, I must proceed on course' " (Lk 13:32–33).

The incident with Herod, however, is much more a personal challenge to the king's evil rather than a revolutionary statement against secular power, and nothing more is said of the conflict until the trial of Jesus. As for Pilate, he is scarcely mentioned in the public career of Jesus. The fact that Jesus would consort with tax collectors and not question their occupation when it was justly executed, the fact that he deliberately refused the title "Messiah" because it would be misunderstood in a political sense, the fact that he avoided all sense of nationalism in the preaching of the kingdom—all this indicates that his squabble was much more in the religious realm with religious leaders, rather than a revolutionary movement which antagonized political leaders.

This is not to say that what Jesus preached had no effect on the social and political dimensions of what the religious leaders influenced. We have just seen his criticism of these leaders in their attitudes toward the poor and outcasts. Nor can we say that Jesus had no qualifications in his support of the state. He *did* criticize Herod. He did speak of worldly rulers who lord it over others. Because of his preaching that the kingdom had a present dimension and that it affected this world reality in all of its social as well as personal dimensions, Jesus' statements had an indirect effect on the secular powers of his time. In the long run Jesus gave the state a relative importance and not absolute. It was only a temporary institution in the face of the coming kingdom. He would not seek its overthrow, but neither would he make it the end-all and be-all.

When finally the Jewish authorities sought to trap Jesus in a political quandary over whether to pay tribute to Caesar, he had a third answer. Give Caesar what is his due, but no more. More importantly, give God what is his due. Moreover, remember that in order to give God what is his due, one will have to make critical judgment as to precisely what is due to Caesar. In other words, the curt sentence of Jesus is probably best understood, not as separation of the two realms, but as interrelation with a bit of opposition: "Give to Caesar what is his, but give to God what is *his*" (Mk 12:17).

This may have revolutionary implications, especially for unjust governments, but it is not the makings of a violent anarchic revolution. Nevertheless, it gives ammunition to the religious leaders who can turn it into a political statement when that becomes the expedient way of eliminating this man who challenged their religious tenets. They will charge at the trial that Jesus claimed to start a kingdom and refused tribute to Caesar. Perfect half truths!

Before we move to the trial, however, we must see the final days. We have considered each of the groups of religious leadership. We have tried to isolate the elements of Jesus' teaching that irked them. We have seen how for each group there was a building up of tension that climaxed in Jerusalem. Now we have but to consider the last few events that seem to have brought all the tensions together and brought Jesus before the anger of his opponents.

Jesus gradually moved out of his semi-withdrawn ministry of wandering around the regions of Galilee. He came to spend the last six months or so in a more concentrated ministry in the Jerusalem area. If John's Gospel may be used to fill in the others, Jesus most likely went down for the feast of Tabernacles in the autumn of his last year. He then remained in the holy city preaching about three months until the feast of Hanukkah in the wintertime. It was during this time that the final battles with his opponents took place, as we have just described them. Undoubtedly two major incidents further precipitated the conflict, even while they filled Jesus with that much more of a sense of urgency and a sense of mission. It seems that Jesus had friends in Bethany on the outskirts of the city and spent time there while he was preaching in Jerusalem those last months. On one occasion, he made a solemn entry into the holy city, accompanied by followers and friends, riding an ass.

Jesus in effect was offering himself as king for Israel, identifying himself in the last days more and more closely with the kingdom of God that he always preached. His disciples proclaimed this for him as they shouted, "Blessed is he who comes in the name of the Lord! Blessed is the reign of our father David to come!" (Mk 11:9–10). Nevertheless, he still would not accept the simple title of "Messiah" because of its political overtones. He made an entry on an ass so that people would see him bringing in the kingdom in humility and suffering. He would not arrive on a spirited horse with military force to drive out the Romans. His kingdom was not of this world, though it was already beginning here and now and had effects on earth.

This spectacular display must surely have attracted the attention of the leaders as well as the crowds, and must have reinforced Jesus' urgent message to repentance and openness to a coming kingdom. Yet Jesus did one thing more to bring everything to a head. Soon after his triumphal entry, if not the very next day, he came from Bethany and entered the temple precincts. He became enraged at the abuse of the temple. Pilgrims were being cheated by those selling them temple sacrifices. The noise of bargaining and dispute in the temple courtyards made it anything but a place of prayer. As Jesus himself shouted, "My house shall be called a house of prayer . . . but you have turned it into a den of thieves" (Mk 11:17). With just indignation, personal authority, and partial approval of those around him, he drove out the merchants and those who dealt with foreign coins in exchange for temple currency. In one swift action he summed up all he had been preaching about the centrality of God's will, his kingdom and the need for genuine inner attitudes and service of the Lord.

This was the blow that brought everything to a swift conclusion. The priests were insulted by his infringement on their territory. The priests, scribes, Pharisees and Sadducees alike, were all infuriated by his implications that their practices and approach to religion were found wanting. A group of them approached Jesus and asked him by what authority he acted. Jesus would not back down, nor would he satisfy their demands. He simply asked them back, "Was John's baptism of divine origin or merely from men?" (Mk 11:30). The authorities obviously could not say that John's popular preaching was merely human. If they acknowledged it as divine, then Jesus had but to say he was carrying on the ministry of the kingdom as John had begun it. Jesus was really asserting once again that his authority was from God and that the religious leaders would simply have to accept that and change their ways accordingly.

From that point on, it seems, Jesus had to withdraw to Bethany. The hostility had reached the breaking point. He spent a month in Perea, east of the Jordan, and then prepared for the final phase of his urgent message about the kingdom. Just before Passover he returned to the holy city. He used the Passover meal to share one last evening of intimacy with his disciples, to affirm again that he would preach the kingdom, and to say that he would, in fact, fast until the kingdom arrived. Then he went out to face the inevitable consequences of his unrelenting and persistent proclamation that God's kingdom was breaking in.

## *Suggestions for Additional Reading:*

Jeremias, Joachim. *Rediscovering the Parables.* Charles Scribner's Sons, 1966.

Cassidy, Richard. *Jesus, Politics and Society.* Orbis Books, 1978.

Cullmann, Oscar. *Jesus and the Revolutionaries.* Harper, 1970.

(*See also the bibliography under the preceding chapter.*)

# Death and Afterward

## Suggested Scripture Readings:

| Matthew | Mark |
|---------|------|
| 26–28   | 14–16 |

| Luke | John |
|------|------|
| 22–24 | 18–21 |

A typical Palestinian tomb with a circular stone door

Nothing stands more important for a Christian than the death and resurrection of Jesus. Still, for that very fact the historical events in their precise details are impossible to uncover. A study of the Gospels makes it unquestionably clear that Jesus died and was buried and that the apostles were changed by an event which they tell us was Jesus' resurrection. However, for the first Christians, the theological implications of the death and resurrection were the important point. They wanted to show that Jesus "died for our sins" and that the resurrection means new life for the Christian. Hence, the stories are told with a great deal of interpretative changes. As we search for the history of the death and resurrection of Jesus, let us see if we can separate the interpretation of the history from the history itself.

As one enters the scene of the arrest of Jesus, two facts seem to present themselves. One is the gentle dignity of Jesus, aware of the mission that the Father has for him, difficult though that may be. The other is the involvement of the Sanhedrin in the arrest of Jesus. We must eventually ask ourselves to what degree and in what way the Sanhedrin is involved, but each evangelist does mention them in some way. Our first impressions are that the hostility toward Jesus is much more a question of a small group within the Sanhedrin rather than an official and open activity of the entire council. We can envision a posse put together on the spur of the moment, sent by hostile plotters, "armed with swords and clubs." They do not even know Jesus very well, if at all, since they need the sign from Judas who must point out Jesus by kissing him. It may well be that the whole Sanhedrin will eventually sit in judgment, but at the arrest there seem to be some who are the more active instigators.

A number of scholars suggest that it was mainly the political sect of the Sadducees who were disturbed with Jesus. They feared that he would disrupt the uneasy compromises they had reached with the occupying Romans. It is interesting, in any case, to note that Matthew and Luke involve only the chief priests and elders as the source of the posse, and most scholars are convinced that even John adds the Pharisees only because they were the persecutors of his own church later on. In other words, the Pharisees were John's problem more than Jesus' problem, at least to the degree that they would plot his death.

The Gospel of John also presents another interesting oddity that has provoked some scholars to give another interpretation to the arrest of Jesus. John mentions that the chief priests "and the Pharisees" sent a "cohort" as well as a detachment of temple guards to the garden. It leads to conjecture that the Romans wanted Jesus arrested and tried. Could it not be that the Romans wanted Jesus eliminated and sent a cohort of Roman soldiers to make sure the chief priests carried out the plan?

It may not be necessary to see John's Gospel as so different from the others in the basic historical facts. It may be, rather, that John simply offers a complementary fact. It could well be that the Sanhedrin, or at least the Sadducees, plotted against Jesus but realized that they needed Roman cooperation to put Jesus to death. Thus, a Roman cohort accompanied the mob, since eventually Jesus would have to be brought before Pilate. An even simpler explanation of the word "cohort" may be that it does not refer to the usual Roman military, but is simply John's way of describing the Jewish police body. This would leave the matter still fully in the hands of the Jewish ruling body and would conform to the basic historical pattern of the other Gospels.

In any case, Jesus continues to be the man aware of his mission, conscious that he had been able to tell that he would be delivered into the hands of others, yet able still to be the man who taught with authority. He would continue to herald the kingdom, wherever that would lead him in his final days and however the Father wanted to bring in that kingdom. Jesus shows this personality even in his arrest as he tells his disciples to put away their swords. Violence will not be met with violence. It does seem that Peter's impetuosity rests again as part of the historical nucleus, as the text recalls that he cut the tip of the right ear of the high priest's servant. John even tells us that his name is Malchus.

In contrast to the gentle strength of Jesus, the story of the arrest gives one final cruel historical fact. The disciples fled in confusion and dismay. When John 16:32 says, "You will be scattered and each will go to his own place," the evangelist could be hinting that the disciples ran back to refuge in their own villages of Galilee. It would take further events to draw them out again. Finally, Mark himself may be hinting that he was also one who fled, being the young man mentioned only in Mark's Gospel who fled the garden, leaving behind the sheet that covered him.

As we approach the scene of Jesus' interrogation before the Sanhedrin, we are left with some puzzles as to the exact historical events. Since the evangelists are more concerned with theological implications of the passion, they are inconsistent with each other in the historical descriptions. Was the trial at night, as recorded by Matthew and Mark, with a second meeting in the morning? Or was there only a morning meeting, as recorded by Luke, and no hearing at night? Was there only an informal interrogation, as John says, and was it before Annas? Or was there a formal trial before Caiaphas, as the other Gospels have it? The questions continue!

We can only speak in probabilities, but the following seems the likely unfolding of history. The hostile party that seized Jesus must have brought him back to those who sent them. It seems quite unlikely that the entire Sanhedrin could have been assembled in the middle of the night. Moreover, it was illegal to hold such night trials. Thus, while it seems likely that some interrogation took place right after the arrest, it would probably have been such as the one recorded before Annas by John. He was no longer high priest, but he had previously held the post and could very easily have been referred to as high priest along with his son-in-law Caiaphas. The hearing would have been to question Jesus about his teaching. It brought the authoritative reply from Jesus that he taught openly in the temple. There was no need to be secretive about his teaching. The high priest had but to ask the people.

The first hearing keeps the consistent picture of the gentle dignity of Jesus and his convictions. It also shows how this is taken to be insolence. The night questioning

ends with a blow on the face from the temple guard and
becomes a prelude to the all-night mockery in prison on
the part of the Jewish policemen, while everyone awaits
the morning activities. This seems to make more sense
than having the mockery follow after the official trial,
when everyone would have been in a position too polite
and proper for such unruly conduct. It would have been
also during this night interrogation and during the time of
Jesus' derision that Peter would have been in the area of
the priest's residence and would have denied Jesus. Once
again each Gospel gives a different version of how and to
whom Peter denied Jesus, but the early Church certainly
would not have kept this memory of Peter had it not been
history.

The morning session now becomes the central hearing, as Luke says. What has been recorded by Matthew
and Mark as a night trial has also probably been taken
from this morning one. As we seek to decipher what actually went on, we are forced to consider more fully the degree of involvement of the Sanhedrin in the death of
Jesus. In all fairness we can be reasonably sure that the
Gospels overstate the guilt of the Sanhedrin. Because of
later hostilities with the Jews at the time of the writing of
the Gospels, and because of the theological concern of the
evangelists to contrast the sins of humanity with the obedi-
ent death of Jesus, the Gospels overstress the hostile rejection of Jesus by the Jews. Perhaps the most striking
example of this is where Matthew changes the crowd into
the whole people of Israel taking blame for the blood of
Jesus.

Nevertheless, the Gospels seem to keep a general
sense of history in imputing major responsibility for the
death of Jesus to the leaders of Israel. The inscription put
over the cross, "The king of the Jews," which is universal-

ly attested and seems historical, appears to be irony on the part of Pilate. It bears witness to what probably transpired in history: Pilate knew that the real reasons to crucify Jesus were religious ones, and that the political excuses were merely presented to obtain the Roman death sentence. There seems plausible argument for not wandering far from the actual Gospel accounts to find the history of the death of Jesus.

In the light of this background we may now return to the official trial before the Sanhedrin. It seems that the religious reasons for condemnation are found here. Whether explicitly or implicitly, Jesus had spoken against the temple and had called for a new order of things. Witnesses came forward to accuse Jesus of this, though they could scarcely keep an accurate description of just what he did say. However, what seemed ultimately to infuriate the judges was the further claim by Jesus that *he* himself would inaugurate this new order. The words of Jesus that we now have to the high priest are surely overladen with the theology of the early Church and represent titles given to Jesus in the light of his resurrection. Still, the conversation might build on basic history: Jesus made unique claims of relationship to the Father that were at least messianic claims and that possibly put him even on a transcendent plane. It was the final point which brought the charge of blasphemy and the sentence of death.

Before we continue our historical quest, we should reflect for a moment on the guilt of the Jewish leaders over the death of Jesus. We must realize again that in the first place we cannot assert this with assurance. Then, even as we deal in probabilities, we must make further distinctions. We are attributing responsibility, not to all the Israelites, but only to those of the time of Jesus, and, even there, not to all the people. The Gospels make it clear that we are dealing with the leaders of the people. It is a small and select group to which we attribute responsibility.

If we have been following the passages carefully, we find that we are not dealing yet with a crowd of people. It is still a small posse and then a closed trial. The mass of common people are not even directly involved, and when they are, they will be swayed by the leaders. As to the guilt or innocence of the leaders themselves, we can make no judgment. How many acted out of hard-hearted disbelief and how many acted out of sincerity at seeing a threat to their religion is not for us to judge. Ultimately, the death of Jesus came because alienation is part of our unredeemed world. The Israelite leaders were simply the last in a line of causality that can accuse humanity at large for killing Jesus.

The next episode in the passion is the trial before Pilate. Some scholars will dismiss the account as unreliable. They claim that it does not show Pilate as the major factor in Jesus' condemnation and as the one to put pressure on the Sadducees to arrest Jesus. It must be admitted that the later concerns of the evangelists to defend Christianity before the civil government led them to soften their presentation of Pilate and the Romans. Nevertheless, there is some historicity in the story as recounted. Pilate did, as a matter of fact, find no guilt in the man. Luke and John stress that point. The Sanhedrin had, to begin with, to change their religious reasons to political ones in order to have a hearing at all. Luke tells us the charges against Jesus were: "We found this man subverting our nation, opposing the payment of taxes to Caesar, and calling himself the Messiah, a king." Nevertheless, Pilate still protested, "I find no case against this man."

Much of the conversation with Pilate, especially in John's Gospel, serves to teach theology rather than simple

history. Still, we seem to have some events which show
how Pilate tried to resolve the trial. He found Jesus to be
from Galilee and sent him to Herod, prevailing on the
procurator's privilege of delegating judgment to a third
person of his own choice. Then he sought to use another
custom, that of releasing one prisoner at Passover as a sign
of Roman benevolence to the Jews. The fact that the other
prisoner, Barabbas, is named lends credibility to this incident as an historical fact. This event also shows at what
point the crowd probably became involved. People turned
out for the release of a prisoner. They were persuaded,
whether by the entire Sanhedrin or by the Sadducees
among the priests and elders, to call for Barabbas and to
have Jesus crucified. Finally, when all these attempts
failed, Pilate turned Jesus over to his troops to be executed. Ultimately, the man who had no love for the Jews re-
lented to their wishes out of intimidation. He already had
enough problems because of them. Now they had threatened, "If you free this man you are no 'Friend of Caesar.'"

The sequence of events involving the mockery and
scourging by the soldiers is also confused in our Gospels.
Did it all take place after the trial, as in some Gospels, or
in the middle, as in others? Most likely it was a bit of both.
It would seem probable that when Jesus was sent to Herod, his own soldiers mocked him and made him play the
king. Then it would have been logical for the Roman soldiers to continue the mockery, perhaps in the context of a
"game of the kings" which they commonly played with
prisoners and traces of which we still find in the archeological excavations of Pilate's house. At this time the soldiers would have placed the crown of thorns on Jesus'
head. Then Jesus would have been sent back to Pilate for
final judgment. Then after that, Pilate would have or-

dered Jesus scourged, not in mockery, but as standard procedure to weaken his condition and hasten his death by crucifixion. The Romans were not keen on having prisoners linger on the cross, so they whipped them as part of the execution of the sentence.

The event of the death of Jesus, being such a significant fact for Christians, is heavily interpreted by the Gospels. Most of the words of Jesus from the cross are probably later additions helping to interpret the meaning of his death for Christians. However, we find strong historical elements as well. The prisoners to be crucified were made to carry the crossbeam on which they would be hung. Simon of Cyrene was made to carry the beam for Jesus after a point in the journey, most likely because of Jesus' weakened condition. That his name has been recorded and his sons, Rufus and Alexander, even mentioned are good hints of historicity. It may also be that Jesus met the women on the road. There was often a group of such women who prepared a spiced wine to be given to the crucified to dull his senses and lessen his pain.

On the cross the end came quickly enough. There is one exclamation from Jesus which seems to bear witness to the fully human, historic reality of his death. It was probably uttered by Jesus, for the Gospels of Matthew and Mark preserve the statement in the original Aramaic, something they do often to preserve the original saying of Jesus. The sentence is, "My God, my God, why have you forsaken me?" These words show the extent to which Jesus went to stand by his convictions. They indicate his distress, his feeling of abandonment by the Father. It does not seem, however, that we must call this a cry of despair. The sentence is part of Psalm 22, which expresses in a real way the feeling of anguish, but also ends on a note of trust and hope.

There seems no reason to deny that Jesus was truly crucified with two other prisoners, that his mother and other women, whose names are not the same in all the Gospels, were present, and that there were bystanders who included the priests and elders, Roman soldiers and passers-by. However, the conversations involving these people have been cast in the theology of the early Church after the resurrection. Finally, we must most likely treat the extraordinary phenomena at the death of Jesus, such as earthquakes and storms, as theological symbols. The death of Jesus was stark and simple at the end. He breathed his last and was taken for a hasty burial before the sabbath sundown.

With regard to this burial there is one last point of uncertainty. Some say the body of Jesus was buried by his executioners as a final act of hostility, and that the careful burial by Joseph of Arimathea was later developed out of respect for Jesus. We do find traces of this theory in Acts 13:29, where it is said that the rulers of Israel, who had Jesus executed, also had him buried. Nevertheless, the naming of Joseph of Arimathea seems to speak for an historical record. Perhaps the best solution is to recognize Joseph as having truly buried Jesus, but not because he was his disciple or the man of saintly virtue depicted in the Gospels. It may simply have been his sense of decency. As a Pharisee he probably was reluctant to join the decision of the Sadducees (i.e., the priests and elders) in condemning Jesus. Now he wanted only to make sure Jesus had a decent burial, as Jewish law demanded.

Had Jesus' death been like any other, the story would have ended there. In fact, there would have been no interest in the story at all, and the Gospels would not exist. As a matter of history, however, one more fact occurred: there was a transformation in the disciples; the men who fled "each to his own place" suddenly arrived on the scene again. The reason they gave was that Jesus was alive, not dead; he had risen.

The event of the resurrection itself cannot be proved and is, in fact, beyond the scope of human history. That is why it is not even described in the Gospels. After the burial the accounts pick up from an already empty tomb. Nevertheless, while the resurrection is itself an object of faith, history can establish the accompanying events. One is always free to give some other hypothesis to explain the events, but at least the events can be established. (And one should note that any other hypothetical explanations remain just as much hypothetical; one makes an act of faith in the other explanations, if one refuses to accept the resurrection as the explaining event.)

The first thing that seems to have happened was the change in the apostles, accompanied by their claim that Jesus was alive. Most likely this basic claim was put forth in the form of stories of angels who appeared and announced the resurrection. The angelic figures are probably theological symbols, but what they proclaim is the point of explanation given by the disciples for their transformation: "Why do you search for the living among the dead? He is not here; he has been raised up."

It seems that this simple proclamation was the first preaching of the disciples, accounting for their change. However, soon after, the preaching became explicit in describing apparitions of the risen Lord. Undoubtedly these served to make the preaching more graphic and to make the truth more convincing for the people. We can recognize that these stories include theological embellishment to interpret the implications of the resurrection for the early believers. The apparitions take place in different locations according to different Gospels, and the stories cannot be harmonized with each other. If they were trying to give just simple historical information we would accuse them of contradicting each other. However, if we take *all* the apparitions *in globo,* without considering details that were altered to make other theological points, we find the common experience of the apostles. Jesus made it clear to them that he was alive, and that it was *really* he, not just their imagination. However, he was changed in some way in a new life, for at first they did not recognize him. When they did recognize him, they knew him to be the same Jesus who died.

Beyond this basic point we cannot decipher how, historically, the apparitions took place. If we were to deal in probabilities, the events may have unfolded as follows. Soon after the arrest, if not after the death, of Jesus the disciples fled to Galilee, with Peter either following after his denial or accompanying them after the death. The major apparition of Jesus probably took place to Peter first, and then to the other disciples while they were reverting to their fishing occupation, convinced that the work of Jesus was finished. This event is contained in some way in the Galilean apparitions in the Gospels. As the implications of the resurrection dawned on the disciples, they put them into the stories of the apparitions themselves. Eventually they sensed the need to establish the messianic community which would be the presence of Christ and they sensed the mission they were to undertake to all peoples. This would have been confirmed when the disciples returned to Jerusalem, probably on the occasion of the Jewish feast of Pentecost, and had an experience of the Spirit which the risen Lord left them. This experience would have been injected into further apparition stories as they became elaborated up to the time of their incorporation into written Gospels. Historically, we may try to formulate this sequence of events. Whether or not we want to *believe* this explanation of the disciples for their change in attitude is another matter and is beyond history.

It is curious that another historical fact has been left to be considered last. Was the tomb really empty? Actually this can be treated last because it is not the central reason for the change in the apostles. The manifestations of the risen Christ changed them; the empty tomb could only be a secondary corroboration. In fact, we have a likely historical reminiscence in Luke 24:12 which says that the empty tomb only further amazed the disciples (and probably added to further fear) until its explanation became clear in the apparitions.

Nevertheless, we do find that historically the tomb was empty. Just who discovered this fact, or how, is again a question of probabilities, for the stories have been edited to include further theological points. They no longer recount just the finding of the empty tomb, but are now joined to the stories of angels who announce the resurrection as the *meaning* of the empty tomb. In digging out the probabilities, however, we hit one strong item. Though each Gospel has variations (two women, three women, or just Mary Magdalene), they all indicate that the women on hand for the burial were the ones who returned and found the grave empty.

Now if the evangelists were simply giving a symbolic story, they would not have used women to discover the tomb, since women were not figures of authority at the time. The fact that the evangelists build around women indicates that they are building on historical facts. The most likely turn of events is that Mary Magdalene went to the tomb, found it empty, and got the message to the disciples. If they were still in Jerusalem they became even more fearful and then fled to Galilee. As they settled in

Galilee, Jesus appeared to them and the mysteries cleared up. If the message of the empty tomb reached the disciples after they had fled to Galilee, then it became a corroboration for what they already knew from the apparitions.

One final confirmation that the tomb was really empty is the story in Matthew about the chief priests and elders spreading the story that the disciples stole the body. It says that even from the start no one could point to the body of Jesus. They could only offer other hypotheses to explain the empty tomb. That leads to a step beyond history and to its interpretation in or out of faith. And that has been the problem and the challenge of the history of Jesus ever since.

## *Suggestions for Additional Reading:*

Sloyan, Gerald. *Jesus on Trial.* Fortress, 1973.

Vanhoye, Albert, S.J. *Structure and Theology of the Accounts of the Passion in the Synoptic Gospels.* Liturgical Press, 1967.

Perrin, Norman. *The Resurrection According to Matthew, Mark and Luke.* Fortress, 1977.

O'Collins, Gerald, S.J. *The Resurrection of Jesus Christ.* Judson Press, 1973.

Brown, Raymond. *The Virginal Conception and Bodily Resurrection of Jesus.* Paulist Press, 1973.

_____. "The Resurrection of Jesus," in the *Jerome Biblical Commentary.* Prentice-Hall, 1967.